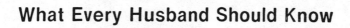
What Every Husband Should Know

JACK R. TAYLOR

WHAT EVERY HUSBAND SHOULD KNOW

BROADMAN PRESS
Nashville, Tennessee

All Scripture references herein are
from The King James Version of the Bible.

Dewey Decimal Classification: 306.8
Subject heading: MARRIAGE
Library of Congress Catalog Card Number: 81-65389
Printed in the United States of America

DEDICATION

TO BARBARA . . .

With regrets that the information herein came so late . . .

With gratitude that you are helpful and patient in the continuing processes . . .

With anticipation that these *now* years are our greatest . . . and getting better!

With my commitment that I will continue to take quality time for implementing the principles of this book in our relationship . . .

PREFACE

How audacious! This is precisely what I am thinking within myself as I embark on this project of writing a book which, in itself, will require a working knowledge of the feminine mystique!

And so I asked myself, *What makes you think that you are qualified to address such a subject?* My mind began racing for reassurance. *There must be a fitting answer! Wasn't my mother a woman? Hadn't I lived with one of these rare creatures, namely my dear wife, for more than a quarter of a century? Hadn't I been witness to our lovely daughter becoming a woman right before my eyes?*

While the answer to all these questions is obvious, the reassurance is far less than obvious. Most grown men in the country could give an affirmative answer on part of the questions. And yet, men's ignorance regarding women is so prevalent that it is a standing joke.

I have heard the adage for years, "Be careful of a man who claims to understand women. He is apt to lie about other things as well!"

A while ago I was in a friend's study and noticed a strange title among his many books. The book bore the title, *All I Know About Women,* and with a shock I noticed that my friend's name appeared on the book as its author. The tome was thick and large, apparently several hundred pages in length. Being an author, and being unaware that my friend had joined the ranks of authorship, I eagerly snatched the book from the shelf and opened a volume of *blank* pages! That about sums up the masculine response to the feminine mystique.

Despite the prevailing conditions, however, there is a direct command in the Scriptures that renders such ignorance both untenable and inexcusable. In 2 Peter 3:7 there is a forthright imperative: *"'Likewise, ye husbands, dwell with them (wives) according to knowledge. . . .'"* I will deal more fully with this significant imperative later on, but we need to know now that it simply means "being properly informed." This being true, I want to state that a knowledge of woman and her needs is not an option or a luxury . . . *but an absolute necessity!*

As I further deliberated this awesome task I came upon a somewhat surprising fact. What little understanding in my mind, which has made this book more of an unavoidable necessity than a personal option, was not so much what I came to understand about my wife, but what I came to understand about myself, my needs, my role as a husband, and my relationship with God! Thus, I discovered what I believe to be a key principle in the marriage relationship—namely, that as mates we can best understand what our counterpart needs and discover how to meet those needs in the light of understanding what our respective roles involve.

In other words, when I find out what I need to be toward my wife, and commit myself to meet the demands of my role, I inevitably learn what her needs are. The illumination has come about not so much by information as by obedience. *What I need to be toward her is what I really need to be. By meeting her needs I meet mine or find them being met in the process.* And the same is true with her, as well as you and yours.

It is toward this goal that *What Every Husband Should Know* is presented—*that husbands might live with their wives "according to knowledge," fully enlightened about the implications of their roles as husbands and fully committed to the implementation of their responsibilities to their wives.*

With excitement, I commend the following pages to your careful consideration and deliberation.

JACK R. TAYLOR

CONTENTS

INTRODUCTION

The Coming Awakening

It is a common consensus among many believers today that our need is a spiritual awakening. Many are committed to praying for such until it surfaces. I am unashamedly among those. Regardless of one's eschatalogical leanings and the knowledge that things are getting worse and worse, God's promises of spiritual refreshings are still valid.

THE PREREQUISITES FOR AN AWAKENING

Essentially, historical revival needs a twofold foundation. First, it needs a *lighting place*, a starting location, a scene where to touch down. That place is often the very spot where bitter struggles are being waged. In the life of an individual it may be amid intense loneliness, frustration, disappointment, or heartache. In the life of a church it may be after (or during) great attack or failure, or in extreme pressure. In the life of a nation it often is during domestic storm, internal division, or international chaos. We learn from the spiritual awakenings of the past that the scene of the greatest struggle and breakdown may well be the very place where God wants to break forth "like the dew" in the land. It is not without reason that the enemy, whose chief aim is to thwart the designs of God, should concentrate his attacks on that exact place where the highest potential for divine good is resident.

Where else but the home is taking place the most bitter struggle and breakdown in our age? Where else but the home is the maximum potential for God's glory to be found on earth? The church is the body of Christ designed to vehicle his divine life, but it will never fulfil its design to any greater degree than is evident in the home!

Second, awakening needs a *track on which to run*. If there were only a place to touch down and no track on which to run, such a mighty power of revival would be *ruinous*, not *redemptive*. Revival is a volatile force. Directed and contained it can work to the good of man and to the glory of God. Without direction and containment there will be dangerous excesses and aberrations. Because of such deviations in past revival movements, many have forsaken their desires to ask the Lord to do it again. This is no more logical than refusing to sleep in a bed since many people have been known to die in them! A move of God is explosively powerful. There is nothing wrong with a directed and contained explosion. The chances are optimum that you today have been transported from one place to another by the means of *orderly* explosions. Your automobile engine is the scene of precisional direction and containment. The same powers turned loose without control would have blown you to smithereens!

I suggest that the home provides the ideal setting for both a place where revival can touch down and a track upon which it can run. Yes, your home and my home! Revival can begin at your address and mine!

I want to include a quote from *God's Blueprint for Family Living* by Howard Hendricks.

Many Christians today are praying for revival in the church, but there will never be revival in the church unless there is revival in the home. And that revival

usually starts with family worship. Richard Baxter, a 17th
century preacher, went to work in an educated, cultured
parish in England. He preached for three years with no
visible spiritual impact. One day he went into his study
and, humbled, said, "O God, unless you move among my
people, I will die." It was then that God showed Baxter
that he had been working for revival in the wrong place.
He had been working for revival in the church, but God
wanted to start it in the home. Then he started going
from home to home in his parish helping families set up
family worship. God began to light revival fires in home
after home that eventually swept that parish and its
preacher to fame. *Today God wants to revive his church,
but this will only happen when the home is revived.*
(JRT's Emphasis)[1]

I firmly believe that Hendricks is right! I will take a step
further and declare that the person responsible for such a
movement has already been designated.

Husband . . . You're It!

The husband has been placed in the position of headship by
the law of God. It does not mean that he is better than the wife.
It means that he is responsible for everything and everybody
within the confines of his home. He may not be directly to
blame for everything that happens, but he is *responsible.* The
abdication of the husband of his headship is doubtlessly the
most destructive factor in our society today. His returning to
headship under the principles clearly set forth in the Scriptures
may be the first significant move in what some historians will
call "The Third Great Awakening."

Yes, husband, you are it! As you view your world falling in
shambles around you, I ask you . . .

If not you, who?

If not there in your home, where?
If not now, when?

Revival in the home, led by the husband, will ultimately mean revival in the church, the business, the marketplace, the educational processes, the government, and the nation.
So may it be!

1
ACCORDING TO KNOWLEDGE

HOW SHOULD I LIVE WITH HER?

Likewise, ye husbands, dwell with them according to knowledge, giving honour unto the wife, as unto the weaker vessel, and as being heirs together of the grace of life; that your prayers be not hindered (1 Peter 3:7).

The above passage is the text and theme of this volume. I will be returning to it throughout to visit and revisit. There will be other passages referred to, but this one will remain central.

This verse contains all that is necessary for a husband to fulfil his role in a manner pleasing to God and sufficient to meet his wife's needs.

It is preceded by six verses directed to the wife. Some insightful soul is bound to ask, "Why are six times as many words given to women as to men?" The answer, I believe, is both intriguing and significant because it suggests one of the things basic to understanding the characteristics of a woman. I will deal with this later, but for your curiosity I will reveal to you that the answer lies, in my estimation, in the basic, unchanging need of the woman for *full* communication.

In this chapter I am set to examine, word by word and phrase by phrase, this vital injunction.

INTELLIGENT TOGETHERNESS

This is what is suggested by the statement, *"Live with them according to knowledge."* Two suggestions prepare us for understanding the husband's role.

The first implication is simply that of *togetherness*. While that appears to be inanely fundamental, it must not be passed over lightly. Most marriages are severely suffering today from a simple deficiency of *togetherness*.

The word in the Greek is *sunoikeo,* from the root word for "house." It simply means to "house together" and denotes domestic association. It is used only this one time in the New Testament.

Not unlike the reference in Genesis 2:24, it suggests an isolation from other associations and a concentration on present associations. Adam said, *"Therefore shall a man leave father and mother, and cleave unto his wife. . . ."*

The second suggestion is that of *intelligence*. A. T. Robertson states that this means "with an intelligent recognition of the nature of the marriage relation."

Togetherness is ineffectual if there is not intelligence involved, and intelligence is superfluous if there is not togetherness in which it can be employed.

Peter is advising, "Live together with good sense!" The average husband may reply, "Well, I think I have good sense, but I don't understand my wife!" You and I need to remember that everything we learned began on the foundation of admitted ignorance. Then there is only one thing to do—*learn!* I have always been of the conviction that Bible command was in itself a promise of enablement. So, if the Bible says I should, I ought. If I ought, I can!

Are you still having trouble understanding that statement, "according to knowledge"? Then, let me pose a question. What would it mean for you to live with your automobile

according to knowledge? Wouldn't it mean that you would
gather all existing information on your car? You would read
the manual.

You would seek to discover what conditions were ideal for
its maximum efficiency. You would find out what kind of fuel it
used, what kind of oil was best, and the care and nurture of its
component parts. You would inflate or deflate the tires according to exact specifications. You would keep your eyes open for
danger signals, listen for strange or irregular noises, and give
proper time for preventive maintenance. The more devotedly
you engage in the above, you are virtually assured more years
of service and more service in the years.

The time is doubtlessly coming when more and more com-
puting will be built into our automobiles. Wouldn't it be interesting if that science were so perfected that our automobiles
could actually tell us what was wrong before the problem sur-
faced and caused a worse problem? That would be the ultimate! Suppose you could climb into your car, turn on a switch,
and have your car reveal to you through a series of lights, signals, or even a voice, just what it needed. If that were possible
and you were sensitive to your car's needs, it would doubtlessly last at least another one hundred thousand miles! And
that will be possible when we can communicate with the
"souls" of our automobiles.

Husband, do you realize that your wife is a fantastic and
sophisticated creature? She is divinely designed for the highest
purposes on this planet or in the galaxies, for that matter. You
and I as husbands are to live with these creations from the
divine hand in an understanding way. How? We can begin
with developing the art of communication. Unlike your automobile, whose inner workings and "soul feeling" you cannot
know, your wife can communicate to you her needs and deep
desires . . . if only you will listen! Through that you will be able
to live with her according to knowledge. The result will be

years added to life—and life added to years!

No man innately understands the deep mysteries resident in womanhood, but as in any field of science he must investigate!

The word used here is *gnosis.* Vine writes that this refers to primarily seeking to know, inquiring, and investigating— denoting in the New Testament, knowledge, especially of spiritual truth.

The husband then is enjoined to learn of the nature and needs of his wife through every existing means, which includes thorough and intimate communication with her. This will prove to be no small task, its size commensurate with the inevitable rewards. It will demand commitment and discipline and will prove to be well worth it!

John Brown said it well a long time ago in clarifying what it means to live with a wife according to knowledge.

> Let him conduct himself intelligently, wisely, prudently. In every department of relative duty, wise consideration and prudent tact are necessary. The peace of the family, the comfort, even the spiritual improvement, both of the wife and of the husband, depend on this holy discretion. This knowledge, or wisdom, will enable him to form a just estimate of his wife's character, of her talents, her acquirement, her temper, her foibles, and will lead him to act accordingly.... Act wisely and the results will be unspeakably advantageous. Act foolishly and there is no saying what the consequences of this, even in one instance, may be. Beware of in any way injuring her; beware in any way being injured by her. SEEK TO BLESS HER, AND TO MAKE HER A BLESSING TO YOU, TO YOUR CHILDREN, AND TO ALL WITH WHOM SHE IS CONNECTED. (JRT's Emphasis)[1]

UNCONDITIONAL LOVE

Admittedly, the word "love" is not found in this verse. Yet, the essence of love is obvious throughout the whole verse.

"Honouring her" is perhaps the most vivid description of love to be found anywhere. This is the essence of love and renders senseless much of what today parades under the guise of love. The statement literally means "to assign honor" or to "to mark off as having great value."

Husband, do you view your wife as valuable? Do you treat her as a treasure? Do you perceive her as precious? To love her is to appraise her as a prized possession, a gift from God.

This unconditional love rests upon two realizations. The first is that the wife is the weaker vessel. The word translated "vessel" seems here to mean "framework" or "fabric." Both man and woman are framework or fabric formed by God. Both are weak, but the woman is weaker. Some women seem to resent this and enter into competition to prove equality or superiority. Such action is doomed to frustration and failure because it is designed to disprove a non-existent inferiority some women feel.

Listen again to John Brown.

> Both in body and in mind some women are stronger than some men; but in ordinary cases, the female, in the human and in other species of creatures, is weaker than the male. In delicacy of apprehension, both intellectual and moral, and in capacity of passive endurance, the woman's mind is often, I apprehend, far superior to man's. But generally speaking, the woman is the weaker fabric. She has a feebler corporeal frame; and her mental constitution, especially the sensitive part of it, is such as to require cautious, kind, and even tender treatment from those about her. Therefore it is meet that her husband should sustain her weakness, and bear her infirmities. . . .
>
> The apostle does not suppose that a Christian husband can be intentionally unkind to his wife; but he supposes that from want of consideration he may do injury in a degree he little thinks, to the one he loves; and therefore

he puts him in mind that his wife is the weaker vessel, and that it is duty to dwell with her "according to knowledge." Very worthy men, not at all deficient in good sense or in good feeling either, but not distinguished by tact or sensibility, need the hint; and a great deal of suffering, no less severe because it is not designed, might be saved if it were but attended to.

It is well to mark how a passing word
Too lightly said, and too deeply heard
Or a harsh reproof, or a look unkind
May spoil the peace of a sensitive mind.[2]

The second realization on which this love rests is that the wife is a joint-heir with the husband of the grace of life. He is to view her as standing on the same level as himself as to the inheritance of eternal life in Jesus Christ. We as husbands and wives in the faith have received together the favor of God which is Jesus Christ himself! Such a view of our wives is bound to arouse our love! When we look at our wives as God looks at them, we see them as precious, and that perception is the foundation of love. Lovelessness is simply the declaration of the depreciation of worth.

"Heirs together of the grace of life"! What a transcendent realization! If this is recognized and spoken of often, then husbands and wives will live as heirs of life and make their earthly state as near like heaven as possible. They will be moved to remind one another of the hopes of this inheritance and to encourage one another to advance toward it with undying courage and hope.

UNHINDERED PRAYING

This monumental passage ends with a sudden and shocking realization, namely, that how we husbands treat our wives can indeed hinder or liberate our praying! Our marital conduct influences the process of our praying! What a sobering thought!

The faults that cause a husband to neglect his wife will also disqualify him for the holy duty of prayer. Until this hour of writing, I had understood that verse to refer to the prayers of the husband being hindered. I have now discovered that the pronoun here is plural *(your prayers)*, and so would refer to his prayer, her prayers, and their prayers together. The whole process of prayer—his, hers, and theirs together—is limited by his failure to comply with what is expected of him as husband.

I feel safe in writing that many a husband who reads these pages will come to the shocking realization that certain of his prayers, and some of his wife's prayers, and some of their prayers together have been hindered because of his neglect in treating her as she deserves as a co-heir of the grace of life.

What I learn, I learn slowly and usually with much agony. It is a usual occurrence that truth has to run over me once or twice before I really comprehend. But after being flattened by it a time or two, I do! The truth of the last statement in 1 Peter 3:7 has been no different than others I have learned.

A PERSONAL ILLUSTRATION

In the not-too-distant past my wife Barbara and I found ourselves in a fresh and intense crisis. The essence of it was the necessity of a geographical move and intense emotional pressures in which Barbara found herself. We tried everything with little relief or improvement. The apparent hindrance lay in the sale of a piece of valuable real estate. We knew that it was God's will that it sell and that we move. But we were not selling it and we were not moving. I tried every rule of prayer that I had ever heard. I sought to believe it was so when it wasn't so it might be so. But it wasn't so! I tried to thank God for it before

I had it so I could have it. But I did not have it! My prayer was simply not being answered. That was the bottom line. I couldn't understand it.

One afternoon, while in a meeting in the Northern part of the country, I was talking with God about this problem and studying it with scrutiny. All of a sudden God brought me to 1 Peter 3:7. I was not a stranger to the verse and certainly had included it in my preaching. But this time the verse was for me. I was shocked.

The Father seemed to be saying to me, "I cannot answer your prayer regarding your real estate until you begin treating your wife according to knowledge." He had my attention for sure. How had I not employed knowledge in living with her? Hadn't I sought to encourage her? Wasn't I trying to effect the move which would remove her from the situation of needless pressure? The answer in each case was affirmative, but still the confrontation was real. "I cannot answer your prayer because you are not living with your wife according to knowledge."

I asked the Lord to specify exactly how I was failing. In my heart again the Lord seemed to say, "You are her protector. You are not protecting her. Her situation is impossible. She feels trapped." I protested, "But, Lord, I am trying to move. I am trying to help. If you would answer my prayer and sell this real estate I could help her." The answer seemed to be direct, "If you would commit yourself to her completely as her protector I could answer your prayer!"

"But Lord, if I moved before that real estate sold I would face possible financial tragedy! I might go broke!"

The Lord gave no indication of sympathy. He didn't seem to care as much about my solvency as about my obedience. Finally, I gave in. "Lord, what do you want me to do?" The reply to my heart was immediate, "I want you to apologize to her and do it my way. I want you to make a move by faith that will put you in a place where if I don't come through for you,

you will go under." Without going into details regarding the apology, I will say that the Lord taught me that one afternoon how to make an apology. He even taught me how to teach her to receive an apology. This is covered to detail in a later chapter under the heading "The Awesome Power of a Sincere Apology." I prepared the apology as I would have prepared a sermon and it required about an hour and a half to deliver it when I finally sat down with Barbara. We wept and loved and planned the move . . . by faith. I told her to select a house and the earnest money would be on hand.

Now keep in mind that for two years we had our place listed with a realtor and had not received one offer. It was a prized piece of real estate. God literally had to work miracles to keep it from selling up until then. When I stepped into obedience it sold within a month and we were moved within two months. My prayers, Barbara's prayers, and our prayers corporately had been hindered by my negligence in living with her "according to knowledge."

A HINT TO HUSBANDS

My dear husband, I am aware that this chapter has been difficult to read. It has not been easily written. But it is vital to the remainder of this volume. Don't leave it quickly. Peruse it again. Learn our text as a memory verse. Read it again and again until you can quote it with understanding.

"Likewise, ye husbands, live with them according to knowledge, giving honour unto the wife, as unto the weaker vessel, and as being heirs together of the grace of life: that your prayers be not hindered."

Exercises for Chapter 1.

1. As you have read this chapter, list the areas that have come to mind in which, as a husband, you have failed to live with your wife *according to knowledge.*

2. Search for any unanswered prayers which may be unanswered because of these areas of domestic neglect.

3. Memorize the text of this chapter (1 Peter 3:7).

2
MAN'S MYSTERIOUS MISSION

THE GENESIS CONNECTION

*And God said, "Let us make man in our image, after our like-
ness; and let them have dominion over the fish of the sea, and
the fowl of the air and over the cattle, and over all the earth,
and over every creeping thing that creepeth upon the earth."
(Genesis 1:26)*

THE ISSUE OF REVIVAL

We have already identified the need of an awakening as the
urgent need of our day. But alas, who knows what it is, what it
looks like, or how to identify it when it comes? We have grown
up with a generation that has never seen revival, except in
small locales. There have been religious aberrations which
have been labeled revival, but the debris in their wake leaves
us wondering whether they did more evil than good. What is
the central issue in revival?

To me the issue of revival is *salvation*. By this I mean that
whatever revival is, it is tied to the very nature of our salvation.
Revival is simply salvation working like it ought to work, salvation up to date. It is the working out of the Christ-in-me and the
Christ-in-you relationships. It is all of Jesus Christ all the time
having all his way in all of us!

But what is the issue of salvation? What does it involve? From what are we saved? To what are we saved?

If the issue of revival is salvation, then the issue of salvation must be *creation*. That is, whatever salvation involves it has a connection to the original intention of God in creation. Then it is vital to understand the Genesis Connection. God created mankind with a purpose. God has made clear the purpose of man in Genesis 1:26. In this verse God "tips his hand" as to the reason for the whole process of creation and all that has followed.

When we have explained the creation purpose, we will have explained the purpose of marriage and the home. For what God made man to do was to be done within the context of the male-female union. We will see how obvious this is in the following chapter when we view Adam's first words as he beheld his new wife.

THEOLOGICAL THESIS

Aside from Genesis 1:26, which is the creation intention, there is no concise statement in the Bible which identifies the central purpose of man in this life.

Man was made for fellowship with God. In one of our creedal statements the suggestion is that man's chief aim is to glorify God and to enjoy Him forever.

Man was made so Christ might have an eternal companion to reign with him in the unending ages of eternity. So believers are making up the "bride," Christ's eternal companion.

While the above facts are true, there is another unavoidable observation. When God created man, Satan had already revealed his capricious and devious heart and had caused rebellion in heaven with the intention of himself becoming the ruler of all. He had been cast out of heaven to earth. Paul calls him "the god of this world" (2 Cor. 4:4) His purpose was to continue guerrilla warfare against the plan and purpose of Jehovah. Satan would use this earth as the headquarters of his campaign.

Donald Grey Barnhouse further clarifies man's purpose in his volume, *The Invisible War:*

> Men have long argued the question at the center of the universe. Some, through tradition, taught that the earth was the center of all things. This is a purely human, if not satanic, point of view. When Copernicus brought out his astronomical system, there were those who opposed it on the ground that it could not be true since they supposed that the Bible depicts a geocentric universe ... a universe that is a circle or a globe of which the earth is the center. But, of course, the Bible teaches no such thing. It goes without saying that the heaven of God's throne is the center of all things, but the material universe, in the sovereign plan of God, was created as a vast theatre to declare the Glory of God (Psalm 19:1).[1]

It is obvious, then, that man is caught in a life-and-death struggle with the powers of darkness, and that man's purpose somehow is tied to this struggle. Barnhouse further explains:

> War has been declared. The great, governing cherub has become the malignant enemy. Our God was neither surprised nor astonished, for, of course, He knew before it happened that it would happen, and He had His perfect plan ready to put into effect. Although the Lord had the power to destroy Satan with a breath, he did not do so. It was as though an edict had been proclaimed in heaven: "We shall give this rebellion a thorough trial. We shall permit it to run its course. The universe shall see what a creature, though he be the the highest creature

ever to spring from God's word, can do apart from Him. We shall watch this experiment, and permit the universe of creatures to watch it, during this brief interlude between eternity past and eternity future called time. In it the spirit of independence shall be allowed to be expanded to the utmost. And the wreck and ruin which shall result will demonstrate to the universe, and forever, that there is no life, no joy, no peace apart from a complete dependence upon the Most High God, Possessor of heaven and earth."[2]

Whatever the purpose of man, then, it involves the settling of the great conflict of the ages between God and His archenemy, Satan. Man is not only involved but is here to represent God in the winning of the war on the visible stage of this earth which has already been settled in heaven. We are thus to pray, "Thy will be done on earth as it is done in heaven."

THE DIVINE DESIGN

Yes, God "tipped His hand" in Genesis 1:26. In no other creation instance was God obliged to delve so deeply into His purpose. He created light and saw that it was good. He did the same with the firmament, the land and sea, the grass, herbs, and trees. He made the sun, moon, and stars and confirmed their goodness likewise. He then created the sea life and the fowls that fly above the earth and the land animals, and also observed that was good. But in none of these instances did he give a reason for their creation.

However, after these phases of creation were completed, God seemed to pause before he made an announcement regarding the coming creation of humankind. He would populate the planet with man and declare His design. Let's observe this grand design.

First, God made humans to be *the extension of the Divine*

Presence. "Let us make man in our image" gives us a hint that man was made to vehicle the likeness of God. What does God look like? I think there is something about us that favors God when we are living righteously.

I pastored for twenty years and learned in the process that one need not say everything he was thinking. This spared me many an embarrassment when I stood with a young father looking into the nursery where his firstborn child lay. Now, to be honest with you, I have never seen too many ravenously beautiful new-born babies. They have been welcomed into the world by a series of traumatic transitions climaxed by a sharp smack on the posterior part of their anatomy. Their first reaction has been a yell with which I am in complete sympathy.

Often their heads are out of shape and covered with either too much hair or hardly none at all. But I found out rather early that there was one statement which was always in order to say. I would look at the little baby, look back at the father, repeat this a couple of times, and philosophically remark, "Bill, he looks just like you!" It was always close enough to the truth to be legitimate. Could the fact that this child, because of the genes and chromosomes of mom and dad, will look like them be a picture of that greater spiritual truth that we are given the spiritual "genes" and "chromosomes" to be like our Father? I think so!

Stay with me. We may seem to be far from our central topic, the home, but we are closer than you think. For we'll see that when we have identified the purpose of the whole human family, we will have identified the purpose of your family and mine.

We were created to show all who observe what God is like. In the final analysis we are worth no more to the world or to God than what our lives show the world of the nature of God. Our success is connected with that purpose eternally. We may succeed at lesser levels, but if we do not succeed at revealing the nature of God to the world we are consummate failures.

You and I were made to look like God. We were made in his image. Our features should remind all who observe us of our Father. Satan should be able to see in our very facial countenances the love and power of the Father. This is at least a part of what it means to be created in the image of God.

Second, God made man to be *the expression of the Divine Person.* The term, "according to our likeness," cannot be taken to be synonymous with the previous term "in our image." Likeness and image are not the same and can be best differentiated by the terms "internal" and "external." Man was made to be like God, not only in his visible features, but in his internal makeup. Among all of God's creatures he alone could express concern, assimilate thoughts, lovingly respond to God, and worship his Creator. He could care, decide, and speak from internal thoughts. God gave him a will which is surely the nearest thing to sovereignty resident among the facilities of man. He could be like God only by having the capacity of volition, the ability to decide. Without this he would be a robot and thus his love and response to God would be either impossible or without relevance.

With this high potential there was also a high risk. Man, unlike the animals, could by his choice soar to the heights of Godlikeness in service and worship. But he could also plummet to the depths of depravity, becoming, in a sense, lower than the animals. Animals are, as it were, locked within their instinctual patterns and unable to go above these patterns or beneath them. Not so with man. By his choice he sinned against God and became what theologians have identified as another species, entirely different from the one God created.

Third, God made man to be *the exhibit of Divine Power.* God made very clear in this verse that man was to have power to rule. He was given dominion to rule over the "fish of the sea, the fowl of the air, and over the cattle, and over all of the earth, and over everything that creepeth upon the face of the earth." God placed the sceptre of authority in man's hand and intended that in everything he did, everywhere he went, he would represent his Creator in ruling over the earth. That rule was to be complete and absolute in every domain. God further clarified this when he later commanded, "Be fruitful and multiply, and replenish the earth, and *subdue* (JRT's Emphasis) it; and have dominion over the fish of the sea, the fowl of the air, and over living thing that moveth upon the earth" (Gen. 1:28).

So man was *designed for dominion.* He was *rigged to rule.* He was *geared to govern.* He was *made to master.* He was *appointed for authority.* He was *selected as sovereign* among the creatures of God.

GOOD, NOT GOOD, VERY GOOD!

Now this is what I want to drive home. As I have described the purpose of the Father in creating man (from Genesis 1:26) I have identified the purpose of the husband-wife relationship. Look with me over the creation story in Genesis 1. The term "good" is used after the creation of light, the division of the land and water masses, and the creation of the sun, moon, and stars. The word is used twice more after the creation of the sea animals and the fowls of the air, as well as with the rest of creation. The word "good" occurs six times before the creation of man.

You know, of course, that God created man as male first. A period of time lapsed between the creation of man and the creation of woman. That is not as obvious in chapter one as it is in chapter two. In Genesis 2:7 we read, "And Lord God formed man out of the dust of the ground, and breathed into his nostrils the breath of life and man became a living soul. And the Lord God planted a garden Eastward in Eden; and there he put the man whom he had formed." In verse fifteen he continues his work, "And the Lord God took the man, and put him in the garden of Eden to dress it and keep it." God then explains the rules of man's reign. His authority is to be contingent on his submission to a Higher Authority. To break this authority will prove fatal. All this information was given before the entrance of woman on the scene.

Then God said a strange and new thing. He said, "It is *not good* (JRT's Emphasis) that man should be alone." It was evident that this was not because man was not good, but that he was not all here, not complete, not able alone to fulfil the intentions stated by God in creation. God was saying, in other words, "Adam, in your present state of aloneness you cannot perform what I made you to perform. You cannot extend my presence, you cannot express my person, and you cannot exhibit my power as long as you are alone. I will create for you an help meet." God was going to give to man one like him to help him and to complete him. This declaration was indicative of the fact that the forthcoming helper was to be of similar nature to man. All that Adam's nature demanded for its completion physically, intellectually, and socially was to be included in this one who was soon to stand at his side. *Thus in man's need, and in woman's power to meet that need, is laid the foundation for the Divine institution of marriage, not only in the first pair in the Garden of Eden, but for all their posterity.*

Immediately after God divulged his intention to create a helper for Adam, He then sent the animals of the earth by Adam for naming. What intriguing timing! Adam's mind must surely have been on his coming help meet. What a shock when the animals were paraded by him. Poor Adam didn't know whether to *name* the next animal or *claim* it. I think, though, that Adam noticed an interesting thing. The tiger had a tigress. The skunk had a "skunkess." The alligator had an alligatress. Mr. Moose had a Mrs. Moose. The Bible thoughtfully explains in verse 20, ". . . but for Adam there was not found an help meet for him." That seems to indicate that he had been prospecting all day long for that help meet.

The rest of the story is history. By God's own hand Adam's side was opened, a rib extracted, the flesh closed in its stead, and finally, the rib, thus removed from Adam's side . . .

> Under his hands a creature grew,
> Man-like but different sex; so lovely fair,
> That what seemed fair in all the world, seemed
> Now mean, or in her summed up, in her contained,
> And in her looks;
> Grace was in her steps, heaven was in her eye,
> In every gesture, dignity and love. (*Paradise Lost* . . . Milton)

God then awakened Adam and brought his new creation to him. Adam had been in the naming business all day long. He would name her as well, and her name would remain as long as man walked the earth. We will view in the next chapter the implications of the statement which followed Adam's first sight of God's fresh creation. Suffice it to say that among the implications was the affirmation of completeness. Adam recognized that she was the affirmation of completeness. Adam recognized that she was present to complete him. Verses twenty-three and twenty-four formed a doxology of praise over the arrival of Adam's help meet.

Now, to complete the picture, look back to Genesis 1:31, "And God saw every thing that he had made, and behold, *it was very good* (JRT's Emphasis)." This is significant. God said six times of his creation processes, "This is good!" He looked upon the aloneness of man and declared, "It is not good!" He presented man with his helper and, *what do you know?* (the connotation of the word "behold") It was very good. All women may take encouragement from this. Before man arrived on the scene it was six times "good." After man was here a while, it was "not good" that he be alone. God made woman and declared that it was "very good"!

THE FULFILLMENT OF GOD'S PURPOSE— A *FAMILY* AFFAIR!

What Adam was designed to do he could not do without woman. So the first wedding was that of Adam and Eve, sanctioned and celebrated by the Living God! Now the combination formed a completeness which could fulfil the commands God had previously made. Now the man-woman combination could extend the presence of God, express the person of God, and exhibit the power of God. They could reign together!

The consummate hopes of civilization are tied to the home, the husband, the wife, and the family. What God would do in his great, wide redemptive plan he would do through the home. There was nothing wrong with the plan. Failure came through man, not because of defects in the plan. There is, therefore, no reason for God to abandon the plan. For this reason the conflict that rages around the home is not merely an isolated conflict of personalities, but a part of the great spiritual battle of the ages between God and the devil. The love between husband and wife is a picture of the love of Christ for his church. The glory of the God-ordered home is akin to the glory of the coming kingdom and the divine family. It is no wonder, then, that the enemy should concentrate his interest in seeking to destroy the loving relationship between a man and a woman within the marriage relationship. For in doing so he will have defaced the clearest representation of God's love to fallen man.

THE FIRST ADAM . . . AND THE SECOND

The first Adam failed in all three of the creation intentions. Having the capabilities to so reflect the grace of God that Adam could have been an *extension of His presence,* an *expression of His person,* and an *exhibit of His power,* Adam forfeited all this and broke with the authority of God. When his submission failed, his authority terminated. He fell. As God had promised, Adam died. He died in his spirit *immediately,* that is, his relationship with God was terminated. He died in his soul *progressively.* He died in his body *ultimately.* Death was to reign completely and universally.

Adam became an extension of his own fallen ego, much akin to the ego-centered archenemy of God, the devil. He became an expression of selfishness and violence. He became the first exhibit of the innate weakness of fallen man and of the power of the devil over the human life.

Then came the Christ! Adam 2! Only from within the context of history could Christ be referred to as the second Adam. For he was long before the first Adam! Examine Christ closely. What do you see? You see the perfect extension of the Divine Presence, the Perfect expression of the Divine Person, and the perfect exhibit of the Divine Power. He not only came to reveal what man ought to be but to die for man, take up residence in him, and rule over him that he might be restored to his true humanity—all this so that, in his restored humanity, he might be so indwelt by Deity that he once again could be an extension of the divine presence, an expression of the divine person, and an exhibit of the divine power. Surely this is the meaning of Paul's statement. "TO WHOM GOD WOULD MAKE KNOWN WHAT IS THE RICHES OF THE GLORY OF THIS MYSTERY AMONG THE GENTILES WHICH IS CHRIST IN YOU, THE HOPE OF GLORY" (Col. 1:27).

HUSBAND . . . WE COME TO YOU AGAIN!

Husband, God is still in business with the same purpose as stated in Genesis 1:26. That purpose is still in motion. It is a plan *affirmed* by the Father, *attacked* by the devil, and will be *accomplished* through man by the Father. You are an integral part of that plan! The home, which is your domain under God, is a picture of his kingdom in miniature, a prototype of his forever family!

The mission of man is your mission now! As you allow Christ to indwell you authoritatively, he will begin to exercise his redemptive powers in bringing the home under his authority, and we may well expect the greatest revival since Pentecost!

The church on earth will never be any greater than the homes which make up its constituency. Revival must start in the home. Husband, you are the head of your home. Revival must begin in you!

Exercises for Chapter 2

1. Read Chapters 1 and 2 of Genesis.
2. Memorize Genesis 1:26.
3. Review the threefold purpose of man contained in that verse.

3
THE WORLD'S FIRST HUSBAND'S FIRST WORDS

"WOW, THIS IS IT!"

This is now bone of my bones, and flesh of my flesh, she shall be called Woman, because she was taken out of Man. Therefore shall a man leave his father and mother, and shall cleave unto his wife, and they shall be one flesh. (Genesis 2:23-24)

On the surface this is a cryptic statement, to say the least. As I was preparing a previous volume, *One Home Under God*, I came face to face with the fact that I didn't have the slightest idea about what this statement involved. Amid that realization, though, was born a suspicion that whatever it meant was vital to understanding the relationship of a husband to a wife and vice-versa. Little did I know what a key it would prove to be!

MONUMENTAL TIMES AND MONUMENTAL PLACES REQUIRE MONUMENTAL PHRASES

Men are known to make historic statements at historic times in the record of man. Lincoln's Gettysburg Address, though in all likelihood more spontaneous than planned, has held the position of an all-time classic. MacArthur immortalized both the phrases, "I shall return!" and "Old soldiers never die—they just fade away." We sent men to the moon a few years ago, and one surely practiced the words he was to speak when he set the first human footprints on the surface of the moon. Thus the now-immortal words were spoken, "One small step for man, one giant step for mankind."

Now, if ever there was an historic time, it was here in the Garden of Eden. What a day it had been for Adam! He had been naming animals all the day long with the promise of God ringing in his ears, "I will make for him an help meet." He had been looking all day for her. Drowsiness came over him, and he drank deeply from the fountains of sleep. During that sleep major surgery was performed by the hand of God. While Adam slept God fashioned woman. It is good to note that the word here is different from the word used for the creation of Adam. In Genesis 1:7 the word is the same used for molding a clay pot. Thus was the creation of man. But when God made woman, the word describing the act was "fashioned" or "hand-crafted." She was special in every exacting detail from the hand of God!

Surely no more monumental a time, place, or circumstance could be imagined than this in which Adam finds himself. He awakens from his sleep and there standing right before him is a creature whose beauty is beyond description. All the latent emotions of his soul are stirred. Surely we can expect an earth-shattering statement at a time like this! Adam stands up to full height, takes a deep breath, and declares, "This is bone of my bones, and flesh of my flesh; she shall be called Woman, because she was taken out of Man. Therefore shall a man leave his father and mother and cleave unto her and they shall be one flesh."

I don't know about you, but after such a build-up, that statement, on the surface, leaves me with a let-down. It sounds to me more like a laboratory report than the romantic overflow of an aesthetic heart! But alas, as I looked at it in the shadow of my ignorance, I began to see some significant hints. Wasn't Adam pure and innocent and filled with the Spirit? Malachi confirms this in Malachi 2:15, "And did he not make one? (Adam) Yet he had the residue (excellency) of the Spirit." I safely concluded that Adam surely spoke under inspiration. Otherwise how was he able even to know anything about father and mother as spoken of in his statement? Without a doubt, the statement is God-ordained. But what does it mean? After exhausting all human resources and finding little reward for time invested, I asked the Lord to reveal the deep implications of this prime passage.

THIS IS IT!

"This is now bone on my bone ..." were the first words of Adam's first statement. The statement as a whole is rather too difficult to translate. I am sure, however, that it is expositionally safe to assume that the whole statement is a word of exciting exclamation. *The Loving Bible* paraphrases the very first words, "This is it!" I am convinced that this is not far from the spirit of the statement. Here is the spur-of-the moment, Spirit-anointed outpouring from within the spirit of Adam. When a man speaks from revelation he always pours out more than he knows. When a man speaks from revelation God has spoken. When God speaks, the statement is freighted with unsearchable riches. His declarations can be examined with expectation because truth always liberates and enriches when it is believed and applied.

Husband, the world's first husband's first words are so significant that without understanding them, you are ill-equipped to comprehend your role and responsibilities to your wife. Examine with me five illuminations regarding this statement.

IT WAS A DECLARATION OF ACCEPTANCE

It would be most difficult to capture the impact and import of that statement in English. That it was no causal, scientific observation is safely assumed. It was the spontaneous, God-directed response of a heart of love in man toward a woman. Though love in word is not to be found in the passage, it saturates the passage in spirit. We'll see finally that every implication studied here is an outgrowth of love. For love, in its essence, is a self-giving quality which causes the lover to seek the highest good in the person loved.

Adam was saying, "I received you, accept you as you are. You are a gift from God's hand, perfect in your presence, and perfecting in your influence on me. You are mine." When I began to realize this my mind almost exploded! I saw a principle that stretched to every relationship in life . . . the principle of receiving or accepting. Adam had a will. With that will he could respond to God, and with that will he could respond to this new creature before him. He willed to received her, accept her. In doing so he released her to become everything God designed her to be. Had the opposite been true—if Adam had rejected her—her fulfilment as to God's design and man's need would have been disallowed. The principle, simply stated, goes, *reception brings release and fulfilment: rejection brings bondage and limitation.*

In years of counseling, I have noted that in virtually every case where a couple has reached a time when coping seems impossible without help, one of the top contenders for enemy number one is *rejection.* It can be passed from generation to generation without deliberate planning, and it can grow in the passing. Rejection is the number-one culprit in divorces and is at the root of all the world's evils. It was rejection in the heart of Lucifer (Satan) which compelled him to seek to lift himself above the stars of God. It was his rejection of divine authority which caused God to reject him and eject him from heaven's hosts. Filled with bitterness and rejection he roams the earth, seeking to inject the poisonous venom of rejection in every human vein. Rejection, perhaps more than hate, is the opposite of love.

In virtually every marriage ceremony are contained the words, "Do you take this woman?" This implies the matter of receiving of the mate with no conditions attached.

I have yet to counsel a couple whose marriage was in trouble in which rejection was not involved. Every marriage is characterized either by *rejection* or *reception*. Where the former reigns, there is divisions, chaos, tension, and bondage. Where the latter rules, there is freedom, joy, fulfilment, and liberation. It is so in a home, in a business, as well as in the church.

This was the first of man's first words, "This is now. . . ." In other words, "This is it . . . wow!" Adam was commending God on a job well done. He was praising woman as his needed counterpart. Every tiger had his tigress, every skunk had his skunkess, and now man had his woman. She was fully and unconditionally received.

Husband, have you received your wife as being God's gift to you? It was no freak of human coincidence that you got together, but a stroke of Divine Providence. You can agree with James that "every good and perfect gift is from above, and cometh down from the Father of lights" (James 1:17). She may not be perfect in your eyes, but you may be looking through the wrong eyes. Look at her through the eyes of God. He sees her as in Christ, his perfect righteousness. He beholds one of the "whoms" of Romans 8:29-30. She is thus foreknown, predestined, called, justified, and glorified. How could you do anything but accept a gift like that? I have known husbands who had no feelings of love for their wives who were challenged to receive them as God's gifts. The result was that, as God's love was released through this act of reception, it became an emotional reality in the heart of the husband.

Remember, husband, as you receive her, you receive all that she is and has. You accept all her personality quirks, all her eccentricities, as well as all her good qualities. That is love. In a real sense when you say, "I love you" and reject your wife in any way, you are simply lying!

Your response to what you would like to see changed in her gives a clear picture of your rejection or your reception. Do you become angry when she reminds you of something you promised to do? Do you haughtily defend yourself when she makes a suggestion? Do you turn her off when she disagrees with you or questions your judgment? When she is in a mood of depression, do you react by silent rejection or absenteeism from the home? You see, when you accept her completely, you will be committed to her fulfilment, regardless of her behavior.

Adam, the world's first husband, exemplifies the spirit of acceptance or reception. As husbands let's follow his example and make this declaration from the heart, "Father, I gladly receive my wife. I testify that you have given me a good gift from heaven. Every quality in her is aimed at perfecting an errant quality in me. Praise you, Father, from whom all blessings flow. My wife is surely among the chiefest!" Then, turning to our wives, let's say, "Wife, dear, I receive you as God's gift, perfecting in my life and a perfect gift from God. I release you to be all that a woman was made to be to a man. I commit myself to you to be all, under God, that a man was made to be to a woman."

After doing this ask God to implement the principle in every facet of your relationship with your wife. Ask him to show where you have been consciously or unconsciously rejecting her. As you view her needs ask God to show you where reception on your part will surely help those needs be met. You likely will see the need of apologizing to her as a result of all you see in the light of this principle. A later chapter under the title, "The Awesome Power of a Sincere Apology" will be of tremendous help to you at this point.

IT WAS AN AFFIRMATION OF COMPLETENESS

> And there these twain upon the skirts of time
> Sat side by side, full summ'd in all their powers,
> Dispensing the harvest, sowing the to-be.
> Self-reverent each, and reverencing each;
> Distinct in individualities,
> But like each other, even those who love.[1]

Adam was saying, as he recognized her as "bone of my bones, and flesh of my flesh," that she was the finishing touch on his glory. If man is the head, she is the crown, a crown to her husband, and the crown to visible creation. Man was dust-refined, but the woman was dust double-refined, one remove further from the earth.[2] "I was not all here until you came. Now that you have come, I am complete. You are the rest of me. Now we can fulfil what the Father ordained us to be and do."

This was obviously a word of faith or knowledge, since Adam knew nothing of past or future. For many husbands it will be likewise a word of faith. You may say it's contrary to prevailing feelings. You might agree at this point that your wife is about to "finish" you but would hate to admit that she is about complete you. But remember, you have the right to say anything that God has said. So say it in agreement with Him. You may have disagreements with your wife. You may be terribly impatient with her deficiencies. You may even have "had it" with her moods, and be perplexed and bewildered at spontaneous transitions from loving queen to wailing wretch. But say it . . . "My wife was sent to complete me. She is bone of my very bones, flesh of my flesh, the rest of me. I am not complete without her." The next thing you know you will be having what you say ... *completeness!*

IT WAS AN ACCEPTANCE OF RESPONSIBILITY

"She is bone of my bone" is a statement which recognizes responsibility. The husband is as responsible for the care and nurture of his wife as he is his own flesh. Adam not only reveals a delight in her character and appearance but a commitment to her welfare. She is not only his possession—she is his responsibility. Her welfare will call him from other duties of lesser importance. She needs him, he needs her, they need each other, and each needs to be needed of the other. With this responsibility comes accountability. We have already seen how a man's treatment of his wife can affect his praying, as well as all other spiritual relationships. The wife, not the business or the church, is the man's chief responsibility after his relationship with God.

The very name given by Adam to his wife was indicative of his responsibility. She was to be called "woman" because she was taken out of man. She began with him. She issued out of him, was derived from him. He is responsible for what comes from him.

Husband, I hold you responsible for your wife. You are responsible for her welfare, for her behavior, and for her spiritual growth. When she shows an imperfection, instead of being impatient and demanding, you should be investigative and inquiring. Where has your responsibility failed? Where have you failed to meet her needs? What can you do to stand in the gap and make her complete? She is yours to have and to hold, to love and to cherish. You and I will do well as husbands to follow suit with Adam and accept our wives as our prime responsibility.

IT WAS A COMMITMENT TO TOGETHERNESS

Before there was a father or a mother, Adam declared. "Therefore shall a man leave his father and mother, and cleave unto her. What a vital rule in marriage! Cleaving is subsequent to leaving. There can be no cleaving until there is leaving. Many a marriage has been undermined and love eroded because of the absence of a leaving which paves the way for cleaving.

The word for cleave literally means "to adhere" or "to stick to." The doxology of Adam in receiving her was not only a statement of approval of what he saw, but a commitment to leave all else and spend the rest of his days with her. That new relationship would have priority over all others. It was not to be an intermittent fellowship, but a continuence of total adherence. They may be part in body for short stretches of time, but they would be together in spirit. It is not without significance that the devil's attack occurred when they were apart. It may well have been in part due to one or the other's failure in cleaving that the opening of the relationship to the enemy's advances came.

Husband, your commitment to togetherness with your wife should mean that you are always seeking reasons to be with her rather than finding occasions of regular absenteeism. It may even be that your job, as mine, requires that you often part with your wife for a span of days. There are ways that you and I can bridge that chasm of absenteeism *if we will*. We can contact our wives every day. We can leave notes. And, above all, we can be sure that when we are with them, we are with them with all our love and interest. Cleaving surely means more than bodily togetherness. It involves aptness of interest, totality of personality, and concentration of affection. More often than seldom such matters as television, business interests, selfish pursuits, and other baubles prevent effectual cleaving between husband and wife.

IT WAS A CELEBRATION OF UNITY

Each fulfils . . .
Defect in each, and always thought in thought,
Purpose in purpose, will in will they grow,
The single, pure, and perfect animal;
The two-celled heart beating, with one full stroke, LIFE!"[3]

Mystery of mysteries is marriage. It defies the logic of mathematics. Math asserts, "One plus one equals two." But God in marriage says, "One plus one equals one!" Adam ended his declaration no less powerfully than he bagan it. "And they shall be one flesh." This was doubtlessly a divine insight of such magnitude that Adam would be glorying in it for 930 years! It must be understood that your simple consent that this is God's plan is not enough. For most marriages the adjustment to this truth will mean serious revisions, most of them beginning with the husband. I jokingly say that for seventeen years of our married life, my wife and I recognized that we were one . . . we just couldn't decide which one. The fact was, we found to be, that it was neither one!

There was not another identity! Before it was just Adam by himself. Now it was Mr. & Mrs. Adam. He died to the old Adam. He could never think, act, or plan as he did before. He possessed a new identity. Before he was "plain old" Adam, but now he was the "Mr." part of a "Mr. and Mrs." combination.

Husband, are you aware that when you attended your wedding, you also attended a funeral? Death is the termination of a relationship. You terminated a relationship with yourself as you formerly were. That person does not even exist any more. You have no right to think, act, or plan as you did before. You died to what you were to become alive to what the both of you were to be in the plan of God. Celebrate, then, your unity!

I further suggest at this point that you commit that first husband's declaration to memory. Repeat it again and again until it begins to yield meaning to your heart. Know that you will have the cooperation of the Holy Spirit as you set His word to your heart. Then begin to ask Him to reveal to you any adjustment you need to make in order to line up with that declaration.

QUESTIONS TO ASK YOURSELF:

1. Am I certain that I have unconditionally received my wife as a gift from God, looking at her through His eyes, and treasuring her as He has?

2. Do I look upon my wife as a means of my completion and have I developed the ability to convey this fact to her?

3. Who is the one person I would rather be with than anybody else in the world?

4. Have I looked upon every situation, especially those in which my wife's needs, feelings, and problems are expressed, as a welcome opportunity to fulfil my capacity to meet her needs?

5. Do I think "aloneness" or "oneness" when I think of ambitions, problems, plans for the future, or have I come to the "we" perspective with my wife?

You know by now that I have merely gone back over the fivefold implications of this chapter and have had you check up on yourself. Now, to keep you honest (and I know you must be interested in honesty), you may ask your wife the following:

QUESTIONS TO ASK YOUR WIFE:

1. What evidences have I given you in our relationship that would convey that I have unconditionally received you? What evidences to the contrary?

2. Have you been made to feel that I look on you as a part of me ... that part of me which completes me? If yes, what means have served to convey this? If no, what have been the evidences?

3. Do you feel that I really enjoy being with you and that I am always looking for ways to have time with you? Do my actions say otherwise? Be specific in instances when you felt that my actions said otherwise.

4. Do you feel that I have a total sense of responsibility regarding your welfare physically, emotionally, and spiritually? Can you remember instances in which the situation seems much to the contrary?

5. What are the proofs inward and outward that make you certain that we are really *one?* What are some signs that may cause you to think that we are not practicing our unity? Would you make some suggestions that would help us both in celebrating our unity?

CHAPTER PROJECT FOR HUSBAND

1. Answer the QUESTIONS TO ASK YOURSELF and keep them to yourself.
2. Predict how your wife will answer each question under the QUESTIONS TO ASK YOUR WIFE.
3. Ask her to verbally give you the answer to the questions, taking notes on her answers.
4. Compare her answers to the QUESTIONS TO ASK

YOUR WIFE to your answers to QUESTIONS TO ASK YOURSELF.

5. Compare the answers she gave to the QUESTIONS TO ASK YOUR WIFE to the answers you predicted she would give on those questions.
6. Discuss your answers, her answers, and her predicted answers.
7. Discuss the variations in your answer and hers and what this means in your communicative processes.
8. Ask her what you could do to improve the relationship using the five points of this chapter:

> DECLARATION OF ACCEPTANCE
> AFFIRMATION OF COMPLETENESS
> COMMITMENT TO TOGETHERNESS
> ACCEPTANCE OF RESPONSIBILITY
> CELEBRATION OF UNITY

....

ASSURANCE:

THE TIME YOU ARE WILLING TO INVEST IN THIS PROJECT WILL PROVE TO BE THE WISEST INVESTMENT YOU COULD EVER MAKE. I PREDICT A 10,000 PERCENT RETURN IN SATISFACTION, JOY, AND THE DELIGHT IN SEEING YOUR WIFE RESPOND TO YOUR WILLINGNESS TO SPEND TIME WITH HER!

....

4
LOVE IS MORE THAN A FOUR-LETTER WORD

SEVEN WAYS TO SPELL IT

Husbands, love your wives, even as Christ also loved the church, and gave himself for it (Ephesians 5:25).

Yes, love is a four-letter word but far more! Have you ever tried to define this illusive word?

Tim Timmons writes in his splendid volume, *Maximum Marriage,* that love is a four-letter word consisting of two consonants . . . L and V, two vowels . . . O and E, and two fools . . . YOU and ME![1]

Someone remarked that life is one thing after another, and love is two things after each other! And the definitions could continue ad infinitum.

Of course, the most well-known statement regarding love is found in 1 Corinthians 13. There is, though, no definition given of love in that chapter. It does contain a significant list of what loves does and does not.

LOVE DOES	LOVE DOES NOT
. . . endure long.	. . . behave rudely.
. . . act kindly.	. . . seek its own.
. . . rejoice in truth.	. . . get easily provoked.
. . . bear all things.	. . . think evil.
. . . believe all things.	. . . rejoice in iniquity.

... hope all things.   ... envy.
... endure all things.   ... get proud or puffed up.

Oh, yes, there are a couple of other things that we must not overlook. *Love never fails! It is the greatest of commodities in time and eternity!*

The word used for this sort of love is *agape*. It is love in its highest expression. Simply defined it is givingness. This will be my working definition for love in this volume.

"For God so loved the world that he GAVE..." (John 3:16).

"But God commended his love toward us, in that, while we were yet sinners Christ died (GAVE his life) for us ..." (Rom. 5:8).

"... I live by the faith of the Son of God who loved me and GAVE himself for me" (Gal. 2:20b).

"Herein is love, not that we loved God, but that he loved us and SENT his Son" (1 John 4:10).

"Beloved, let us love one another; for love is of God; and every one that loveth is born of God, and knoweth God. He that loveth not knoweth not God; FOR GOD IS LOVE" (1 John 4:7-8).

With this as a background, let's observe what a husband is supposed to mean when he says to his wife, "I love you."

Love is more than a four-letter word. It may be a five-letter word or even a thirteen-letter word. The reason for these variations is that love in reality is not as much something you *feel* or something you *say* as much as it is something you *do*.

Let's note some variations in the spelling of L-O-V-E.

Love May Be Spelled A-W-A-R-E-N-E-S-S

Among the needs of a wife is that of sensing that she is thought of, noticed, and appreciated. A male habit seems to be preoccupation. There is no such thing as love without awareness. The very essence of love is givingness, and givingness requires an object. Having an object of love requires awareness.

Husband, are you continually aware of your wife? By that I don't mean to suggest that it is possible to have her in the forefront of your mind every hour of the waking day. I do suggest that it is possible to be aware of your wife in a manner satisfying to all of us.

There are two factors to be considered in the matter of awareness. The first is that of *developing* awareness in our own minds pertaining to our wives. The husband who lives with his wife according to knowledge is one who has committed himself to a life-study of her nature and needs. This study will be of such a nature that unawareness will be an impossibility. A husband who prays for his wife regularly will be regularly aware of her.

Fellows, most of us as males are unmindful by nature. It we admit this we can develop deliberate projects geared to change our approach. For instance, have you noticed what dress your wife has worn the last three outings (if there were any outings!)? Did you say anything complimentary to her about her apparel? Have you lately said anything to her about her hair-do? (favorably, I mean) Only a few minutes a day will greatly increase your A.Q. (Awareness Quotient) I will list more projects at the end of this chapter.

After developing awareness of our wives in ourselves, we need then to plan deliberately how to let our wives know we are aware. It is one thing to be aware. It is quite another to *convey* that fact to your wife. I will discuss later on why such a project can mean so much to your spouse. It is directed toward one of her basic needs. No investment will yield more returns than those moments spent in developing an awareness of our wives and in developing visible and vocal means of evidence to them.

Love May Be Spelled T-I-M-E

A husband is usually an extremely busy man. The hours of his day are like dollars in a bank account. His commitments are the checks he signs to withdraw the deposits of hours in his day. He inevitably spends his time doing what he considers to be of priority quality. Much of his time is consumed by matters within the scope of his work. Over these he has little choice. They are like the regular monthy bills—he just pays them. But the husband has periods of time when he does have jurisdiction over how he spends those periods. How he spends those times communicates much about what is really important in his life.

In days of courtship time was a dominant factor. There is something about a first love that almost renders the use of the clock or watch out of date. Valuable time was spent sharing, planning, and simply being together. There were other things to do, but nothing was really more important than being together. A five-minute journey to the convenience store could stretch into an hour. And whatever the time we were required to come in was too early. True love never seems to get in much of a hurry.

In most marriages time is also a pivotal factor. There seems always to be a shortage of it. Times of sharing and pleasure are sacrificed on the altar of business expediency. It's the demands of school, business, or the favorite television programs. The home becomes headquarters for a multiple business rather than a place of sharing and togetherness.

Husband, when you tell your wife you love her, it is most difficult for her to believe it when she sees you choose to spend hours over which you have jurisdiction in doing other things than tending to her needs. In the final analysis, the measure of your love may be understood by her to be commensurate with the amount of time spent with her or in pursuit of meeting her needs. Now it needs to be stated here that many husbands really do not have many hours of this nature to spend. This is generally not a problem with an understanding wife when the husband is willing to spend *quality* time out of the little that he does have.

At this point the significance of a little word should be observed. "With" denotes association and is of vital importance in this discussion. It is not enough to spend time *around* our wives, or even *near* our wives. We need to spend time *with* our wives. And there are times when it is absolutely necessary to spend time with them exclusively.

Every now and then a husband needs to plan into his schedule an evening, an afternoon, a day, or a weekend devoted for his wife. Never will he say "I love you" and be heard any clearer in the heart of his wife. On the other hand a husband may say, "I love you" regularly and find that statement neutralized by his time priorities which say, in essence, "I have no time for you."

Love says, "I want to be with you. *I will find time!*"

Love May Be Spelled T-A-L-K

I will deal more fully with this later in a chapter on communication. It may be helpful to remember an adage which is much more than a clever phrase:

Love for Continuation Depends Upon Communication

Are you aware that one of the most often-heard complaints from modern wives against their husbands is, "My husband never talks with me!"? We are beginning to see a pattern which reveals that love never merely loves and leaves it at that. It loves *and* gives, or loves *and* comes, or loves *and* tells, or loves *and* works.

It is not without meaning that, in Paul's incisive passage (in Ephesians 5) on the husband and the wife and Christ and the church, he said (in verse 26): "that he might sanctify and cleanse it with the washing of water by the Word." This is more than an implication that communication cleanses like a detergent. Communication is doubtlessly the cleansing agent in the marriage relationship.

The ancient art of conversation has almost become a lost art in our culture. Blessed is the husband who will take the lead in reviving and preserving it.

Love says, "I am willing to talk with you."

Love May Be Spelled P-R-A-I-S-E

Praise in the biblical sense is visible, vocal, or audible adoration. It required either the use of the body (dancing, clapping, or hands raised), the voice (singing or speaking), or instruments of music. We are told that God finds praise "comely" (good-looking, commendable) in the upright (Ps. 33:1).

A woman never tires of hearing praise. This is another exercise which speaks to a basic need of a wife, that of a constant need of visible and vocal reassurance that she is loved. A little praise at the right time will go a long way.

Technically, there is a difference between thanksgiving and praise. Thanksgiving or gratitude generally have to do with things while praise has to do with persons or personal traits. We thank God for things. We praise God for his personal attributes. Though thanksgiving is never out of place, praise is the premium quality of the two. Praising someone requires evaluation and response, as well as communication.

While it is helpful to compliment your wife on her manner of dress or how she cooks, it is even more helpful to praise her for a personal characteristic such as thoughtfulness or patience. When she listens to you praise her, she hears much more than you are speaking. She hears you indicate that you are aware of her, that you have taken time to consider her traits of character, and that you cherish her as a person of value.

Your wife will find personal satisfaction when you thank her for ironing your shirts or cooking your breakfast, but she will find infinitely more joy in hearing from your lips what a splendid wife or mother she is.

Love May Be Spelled L-I-S-T-E-N

Dr. John Drakeford suggested the centrality of this area in the title of his book, *The Awesome Power of the Listening Ear.* Indeed there is awesome power in the art of listening! Logic should teach us that we should listen at least twice as much as we talk. After all, we have *two* ears and only *one* mouth!

Another often-heard complaint from wives is, "My husband never listens to me!" The art of ignoring is almost unsurpassed among married couples today. Husbands seem to have a knack in developing the art and become quite adept as ignorers!

Husband, your awareness of your wife's needs and welfare will dictate the necessity of two kinds of listening. The first is *casual* listening. You need to be listening all the time to hear the little things vital to the fulfilment of your wife. This kind of listening will pick up voice tones, key words, moods, and other important factors in a relationship. Second, there is *concentrated* listening. You may casually listen while you read the paper or eat your meal. Your ears may receive many sounds at the same time. There are, though, times when you must have ears only for your wife's words. Your body, soul, and spirit must be concentrated in this all-important endeavor. She needs to know that you are listening, not only with your physical ears but with your soul and spirit. Her most comforting assurance at times will be, "I was heard!"

Love says, "I have the time and interest to listen to you."

Love May Be Spelled C-O-N-S-I-D-E-R-A-T-I-O-N

Consideration is an intangible commodity. It's sort of like "unction." When the preacher was asked what unction was, he thought about it a minute and replied, "Well, I don't know what it is . . . but I know when it ain't!" The same is true with consideration. It may be difficult to define, but it is not difficult to recognize it's absent!

Consideration is defined in the dictionary as "thoughtfulness for others and their feelings; regard; respect."

Leo Tolstoy, the famous Russian writer, was always talking about living a life of love. But his wife wrote poignantly of him. "There is so little genuine warmth about him; his kindness does not come from his heart, but merely from his principles. His biographies will tell how he helped the laborers to carry buckets of water, but no one will ever know that he never gave his wife a rest, and never in all these thirty-two years, gave his child a drink of water or spent five minutes by his bedside to give me a chance to rest a little from all my labor."[2] What a sad benediction to a supposedly successful life!

Nothing has helped me more in this area than taking time to deliberately try and move to my wife's viewpoint in life and look at life from her perspective. She would tell you (and I would have to agree) that for the first years of our marriage I was a grossly inconsiderate person. I am improving! God will be obliged to help us understand other people's points of view (especially our wives) as we continuaously pray for them.

Love says, "You register in all my considerations."

Love May Be Spelled T-O-U-C-H

The importance of a mere touch is often overlooked. You may have heard the story of the couple who married. After a whirlwind courtship they began their days of life together. She had noticed that sometimes he was less than affectionate, but it seemed not to matter. Gradually her vivacious and vibrant personality began to change. She began to be quiet, sometimes morose and depressed.

Finally she virtually lost her personality and assumed a zombie-like appearance. Only then did the young husband attach enough seriousness to her state that he would seek to communicate. But there was no communication. She would simply stare into space, never smiling, never responding. He carried her to counselor after counselor with no change apparent.

Finally he took her to a much-recommended counselor whose record was enviable. Several sessions witnessed no response. Finally, in what was scheduled to be the last session, the counselor laid down his pencil and pad, got up from behind his desk, and, right in the presence of the husband, tenderly reached out his hands to the wife, caressing her cheeks in his hands and planting a kiss on her right cheek. The effect was electric and sudden. She blinked three times, a bright smile illumined her face, she began to talk excitedly, and her vivacious personality was back! Her husband was dumbfounded but glad. He drew the counselor aside and asked what caused the change. The counselor confided that she was just starved for affection, and he would recommend the same treatment at least every Monday through Friday. The young husband replied, "Well now, that would be fine except that I don't believe I could get her here on Fridays. That happens to be my bowling day!" He had totally misunderstood. The story would be much more humorous if it were not so close to home.

Happy is the husband (and happier is his wife!) who learns the place of thoughtful affection at the right time. There is something in a touch that conveys volumes of words.

Love says, "I need to touch you, to sense you, to let you

know that I am here, and I am aware that you are there."

These are only a few variations in the spelling of love. How do you spell it? However you spell it, show it! It is expressed well in the little song:

> A song is not a song until you sing it,
> A bell is not a bell until you ring it,
> And love is not love until you give it away.

Would you like to implement the discussion of this chapter with a project? Let me suggest the following:

A SEVEN-DAY LOVE PROJECT

First Day
1. Give yourself a "love" test, using the seven things that LOVE DOES and the seven things that LOVE DOES NOT (at the first of the chapter).
2. Evaluate your A.Q. (Awareness Quotient) and plan awareness projects. Today notice everything about your wife that you possibly can, such as dress, make-up, hair-do, and the like. Spend a few minutes at the beginning of the day praying for her. Give her a call from the office or wherever you are. The word for today is A-W-A-R-E-N-E-S-S.

Second Day
1. The Word today is T-I-M-E. Give your wife some of it!
2. Plan to give her thirty minutes today of *quality* time. (Nothing else planned, you are hers completely!)
3. Today take some time to fix something around the house that has been a subject of past discussion.

Third Day
1. The word today is T-A-L-K. Do it!
2. When you get home today take some time to *talk* with your wife. She is interested in every detail! Tell her about your day.

Fourth Day
1. The word today is P-R-A-I-S-E. Start the day with it!
2. Leave your wife a note somewhere so she will find it shortly after you leave for work (A note of praise for a personal character trait you see in her!).
3. Deliberately plan to think about your wife several times at work and word some evaluations that are praiseworthy about her.
4. When you get home share one of these with your wife.

Fifth Day
1. The word today is L-I-S-T-E-N.
2. Check your listening habits today at home and elsewhere.
3. Ask your wife if you are a good listener. Request her to suggest how you might be a better listener.

Sixth Day
1. The word today is C-O-N-S-I-D-E-R-A-T-I-O-N.
2. Plan to help her with the dishes or cooking at least one time today.
3. Give her a gift, flowers, or candy. Remember, love is *givingness.*
4. Plan one thing today to let her know that you often think of her and her situation and know how she feels.

Seventh Day
1. The word for today is T-O-U-C-H.
2. Give your wife a back rub today (or perhaps a foot massage!)
3. Practice physical gentleness deliberately.

PRESCRIPTION:
If the above works to make a happier home, keep it up until you are habituated!

5
THE DEMANDS OF HEADSHIP

A POWERFUL POD OF P'S

But I would have you know that the head of every man is Christ; and the head of the woman is man; and the head of Christ is God (1 Corinthians 11:3).

Order is heaven's first law. Nothing exists for long without order in an unchanged state. Depraved man has considerable difficulty in understanding this, and even more difficulty in implementing it. Failure to heed this existing order established by the Creator has been the source of earth's chaos and heartache. Mankind is still trying to prove that there are no absolutes, that people can really do as they please, and all will be well, but his record does not speak well of his attempts.

We are always wanting to argue, "Well, that is not the way I see it" or "I just don't agree with that." It would be good to remember that an essential definition of truth is simply—what God says. That is truth when you don't agree with it. It is still truth when it does not make sense to any of us. It is truth when the devil lines "logic" up on the other side to make us doubt.

With good intentions I used to say, "God said it, I believe it, and that settles it!" I have learned better, later. Now I know that God said it, and *that* settles it, *whether I believe it or not.* It is not my believing that settles it. God's Word was settled long before you or I came onto the scene. "Forever, O Lord, thy Word is settled in heaven" (Psalm 119:89). Now the truth is that if I want it to be settled in my heart, my believing settles that!

We come to discuss the matter of headship and its demands. The husband is the head of the wife. This is an outright biblical statement. Rejected by many, opposed by more, believed by some, and practiced by a few, it remains a bone of contention in almost every era.

The model by which we come to understand and implement the headship of the husband is that of Christ. The two facts are linked together. The head of every man is Christ, and the head of the woman is man. In every situation, be it household, business, or church, there must be authority and submission. Somehow we have come to have unreasoning phobias about the words "above" and "beneath" when it comes to authority. But the very existence of laws presupposes something or someone behind those laws who established them. Laws are useless without a system of *responsibility* and *accountability*. It is not bad to be "beneath" if what is "above" gives us shelter, safety, and provision. It is entirely advantageous if, through this system of "aboves" and "beneaths," we can keep our existence related to God in such order. That is the precise design of the whole system of law, authority, and responsibility.

The design of the law is not bondage, as some would suppose, but freedom of the highest calibre. The headship of both Christ over man and man's over woman properly understand and practiced will lead to liberation the likes of which will never be witnessed by all the liberation movements of every generation.

In this headship the three important words are *authority, responsibility,* and *accountability.*

The head of the woman is man. This is a fact notwithstanding that many men are base and unworthy of their position

and calling; notwithstanding that many women are pure, but
. noble and well-fitted for command. We shall never understand
the headship of God over Christ until we heed to the headship .
of Christ over man. When we implement the entirety of total
headship we shall see that our earthly relationships are but the
means to bring us into line with God himself and the whole
spiritual flow of the universe.

"Let there be non-conformity with this, and there is discord
breaking in upon the harmony of the spiritual universe. Let
there be conformity, and the sweet concert proves that earth is
in touch with heaven."[1]

For the remainder of this chapter I will deal with the demands of this headship of the husband in relationship with his
wife. Our model again will be none other than Christ. The husband is to love his wife *as* Christ loved the church and gave
himself for it. That little word "as" connects all the implications
of the love of Christ with our responsibility as husbands.

HEADSHIP DEMANDS PROVISION

Christ died for the church and through that death provided
life for the church. He is the head of the husband. Thus, the
husband is to die to single life to provide life for a new identity
... two who have become one. The husband, to his wife, is the
embodiment of all that Christ was and is to the church. The
wife and the family are uniquely the husband's responsibility.
Our society has little trouble realizing a part of this. But beyond
a primary realization that is quite cultural in context, our blind
spots are massive.

THE PROVISION OF SECURITY

Our culture recognizes the validity of this expectation. The
Word of God makes crystal-clear the severity of failure to provide for one's own. "But if any provide not for his own, and

especially for those of his own house, he hath denied the faith, and is worse than an infidel" (1 Tim. 5:8).

It would be difficult to imagine any infraction more severe than this. Almost any culture holds the man responsible for the physical provision of his own and is quick to unsheath the sword of justice in cases of deliberate, wanton neglect. It might be fearful, however, to look beyond this to other provisions that this verse may imply.

THE PROVISION OF IDENTITY

The Lord Jesus gave identity to us as the church in time and eternity. When husband and wife are joined they become "Mr." and "Mrs." She took his name. Husband, your wife has given up the name of her birth for yours. She has tied her identity to you. She will have (or has) borne you children who will likewise bear your name. You have given them a basic necessity—an identity. More important than a title, however, is the character that is a part of your gift to them. They will not only possess your name—they will likely possess your character.

THE PROVISION OF UNITY

As Christ is the "fulness who fills all in all," so the husband is the center of the home. The word for husband comes from a German word which means "house band," or the one who holds the home together.

THE PROVISION OF DESTINY

Our Savior and Head provides the church with destiny. So the husband provides destiny for his family. It is noteworthy that Joshua stressed, "As for me and my house, we will serve the Lord" (Josh. 24:15). I believe that Paul understood this principle when he said to the Philippian jailer, "Believe on the Lord and thou shalt be saved, and thy house" (Acts 16:31).

HEADSHIP DEMANDS PROTECTION

As Christ died to provide life for the church, he lives to protect his investment. He lives to protect that which, by his death, he purchased.

The husband is the protector in the domain of the home. The whole spiritual world recognizes this protectorate. A husband, indwelt by the Spirit of Christ and under the Spirit's control, will create a protective atmosphere around his home that will be recognized by the hosts of hell. This is protection without limitation. It includes physical, social, spiritual, and emotional aspects. It is a fact without argument that where there are homes within God's order, there is little emotional or mental illness. The demons of hell mark well the household guarded over by a godly husband!

HEADSHIP DEMANDS PRIESTHOOD

Jesus Christ continues his relationship with the church, not only from within her as its life, but as an intercessor in heaven—". . . seeing that he ever liveth to make intercession for them" (Heb. 7:25). He is the high priest of our profession (Heb. 3:1). While every member of the family has the right to approach God for himself or herself, the husband has the unique right to represent his whole family at the Throne of God. How it must delight God to see the head of the family coming to Him with the needs and pleas of the entire family! Husband, you have no higher responsibility than to represent your family in prayer. If taking time to earn a living—which puts food on the table, clothes on their backs, and shelter over their heads—is worthy, of how much more worth is that time spent in ministering to them before the Throne of Heaven? In prayer we transact divine business which hedges our children in to the will of God all the days of their lives. God, help us to take our priesthood seriously!

HEADSHIP DEMANDS A PROPHETIC ROLE

A priest is one who goes to God on behalf of man. A prophet is someone who comes to man in behalf of God. The husband is a "resident prophet" in his own household. It is both his privilege and responsibility to provide spiritual direction for his household. He "forthtells" the word of God to his family, thereby giving them things he has learned and heard in the prayer closet in priesthood. He will come out to share in the office of prophet. Thus will divine guidance be given for the family, and divine order will assure divine blessings.

HEADSHIP DEMANDS PROFESSORSHIP

The home is the classroom where more is to be learned by its occupants than anywhere else in the world. Jesus, through his indwelling Spirit is "teaching us all things" and "bringing all things to our remembrance" (John 14:26).

More and more should the father and husband assume the role of teacher in the home. If the day existed when we could rely on the public education system to teach our children moral values, that day has gone forever. Though he may not hold regular classes, the godly husband-father will teach his wife and family.

The average American family spends more than twenty hours per week sitting at the "feet" of the most effective teacher in our culture, the television set! More and more, then, must the husband stand in the gap to instruct.

HEADSHIP DEMANDS PARTNERSHIP

We are heirs of God and joint-heirs with Christ. We are partners as husbands and wives of the grace of life. Partners view the business as partners. Their attitude toward each other is that of concern because what effects one effects the other. All can be shared *together*. We are partners *together*. What a wonderful thought—*together!* I remember when my wife and I faced the loss of our first baby. We had shared *together* the anticipation of his coming! We would face the crisis of his passing *together*. I would not want to think of how it might have been had we not been able to go through the experience *together*.

With all these demands we tend toward bewilderment as husbands. I have bad news and good news. The bad news is that you and I cannot do it! The good news is that He can. For whatever he demanded of us, he is in us to enable the doing of it! There is a final consideration with which I want to close this chapter. It does not come under the category of a demand but rather a privilege. The husband needs to be a friend to his wife. In that memorable chapter of Song of Solomon 5 the country maiden describes her lover upon the request of the women. She crowns her vivid description with this vital word, "This is my beloved and this is my friend" (5:16).

Project Suggestions for This Chapter

1. Husband, grade yourself in each of these areas A,B,C,D, or F.

_____ As Provider
_____ As Protector
_____ As Priest

_____ As Prophet

_____ As Professor

_____ As Partner

_____ As Pal (Friend)

2. Suggest to yourself how you may implement the demands of your role in each particular area.

3. Make a project of becoming a better friend to your wife.

6
THE AWESOME POWER OF A SINCERE APOLOGY

LIFE'S THREE HARDEST WORDS

ON THE APOLOGY...
An Apology is a friendship preserver, an antidote for hatred, never a sign of weakness. It costs nothing but one's pride, always saves more than it costs, and is a device needed in every home!

—Anonymous

Our subject in this chapter will be the apology. In the middle of this writing I was asked, "What would you suggest as the first thing a husband should do in order to live with his wife according to knowledge?" I mused a moment and replied that I thought the best thing a husband could do would be to start apologizing. Now, that may seem to you a little hasty, tending to overgeneralizing. I have thought about it since and am more convinced that the spur-of-the-moment answer was right on target.

So the expected reaction of the husband-reader would be, "Why, what have I done? I know nothing I need to apologize for to my wife!" I would hope that as you have read the first chapters of this volume God has already shown you some areas where relationships need to be righted.

To the above expected reaction of you, husband friend, I share this story. In my particular denominational persuasion

71

there is a word which categorizes a decision called "rededication" which many make during invitation times. In all the years
of my growing up I never had anyone define it, speak of its
involvements, or give instructions on just why or how and
under what conditions it should be made. So I grew up sup-
posing that when nothing else would work to improve one's
relationship with God, rededication would. I guess I looked
upon rededication as sort of an apology to God. To be perfectly honest with you, I do not remember deriving much long-
term benefit from the "rededication trip." But during the early
years of my Christian pilgrimage, rededication was sort of a
semiannual ceremony (at least). But I heard a story that so
closely characterized me that it exploded the "rededication
myth."

It seems that there was a certain preacher who insisted that
when a person came down the aisle to make a decision, they
should have something clear in their minds that was to happen. One Sunday morning a young man came down the aisle
with a few modest signs of repentance (at least he was misera-
ble) and said, "I am here to rededicate my life!" Immediately,
without batting an eye, the preacher said, "Well, young man,
confess your sins and get right with God!" The young man was
surprised and shocked at the preacher's forthright approach.
His reply was, "Sir, I can't think of any sins right now." The
preacher was as fast on the reply, "Well, young man, just start
anywhere and guess at it!" Do you know that this young man
did exactly that and guessed right the first time!

Husband, that story conveys what I want to say to you right
now. Do you want an improvement in relationships at your
house, especially between you and your wife? Then begin with
an apology. You ask, "I can't think of anything for which I
need to apologize." My reply to you is, "Just start anywhere.
The chances are very good that you will guess right the first
time, and it will all be light and downhill from there!"

THE DERIVATION OF THIS INFORMATION

The information in this chapter came from the heart of the Lord to my heart one afternoon as I sat in my motel in the cold Northland of our nation. I partly shared this in the first chapter as I described the situation with my wife and our crisis. It was a painful afternoon as the Lord convicted me that I had violated my wife's welfare, because I had not given her the protection that is the husband's responsibility. As this conviction came I asked the Lord what he would have me do. This was when he began to teach me about an apology.

Seldom had my wife heard me speak those three hard words, "I was wrong!" Less frequently had she heard me explain where I had failed with promises that "things will be different." For hours I sat at the feet of the Teacher as he taught me a definition of an apology, the demand for an apology, the design of an apology, and the dynamics of an apology. The more I learned, the more I saw that I must apologize to my wife. Though I talked with her on the phone, I couldn't do all that needed to be done by long distance. It must be done face to face. So, in a few days, at my next engagement I apologized to her for more than an hour and a half! I will get into the structure of the apology later because I am sure that the reader is perfectly mystified now, wondering how anyone could make that much of an apology to fill an hour and more.

THE DEFINITION OF AN APOLOGY

The apology is defined as "words saying one is sorry for an offense, fault, or accident; an explanation asking pardon." It is a statement of recognized offense revealing willingness on the part of the one making it to straighten things out. It is not a sign of weakness but a sign of strength of the highest sort. It is the capacity of the human will to recognize, repent, and make restoration to rebuild human relationships, as well as divine relationships. Apologies are the deep pilings upon which a strong foundation of relationships can be laid.

Without the apology a relationship remains a surface relationship. When there are conflicts that do not result in an apology from one or the other (or both), that relationship is destined to remain shallow, never deep, and seldom meaningful. In our relationship with God the apology is simply confession of our sins. It is honesty verbalized. It is defensiveness becoming open. It is pride taking off its mask. It is the most psychologically disarming action a human being is capable of taking. It will work when nothing else will. It is the highest-powered detergent in a human relationship.

Our discussion of an apology will be primarily from the standpoint of husband to wife. The fact is, though, that most of the rules would apply to wife to husband apologies as well.

THE DEMANDS FOR AN APOLOGY

As we'll see later on (in the chapter on communication), there must be a starting point for effective communication. For many married couples that starting point will be the apology. For most of these it will specifically begin with the husband. He is the one responsible. That being true, a better state of affairs will likely begin with the husband beginning to make adjustments.

The apology is called for to clear the air and pave the way for constructive communication regarding problems which impede success in the marriage relationship. It is the white flag lifted over the battlefield, and it demonstrates willingness to negotiate undefensively.

An apology is helpful in putting down the weapons of attack and laying down the shields of defense. The giving of an apology represents the sublime aquiescence of a loving heart, and the acceptance of an apology assumes love's omnipotent ability to forgive.

Above everything else that an apology does in a relationship is this—*it opens the matter to the Spirit of God who sheds abroad in our hearts the love of God.* There is something supernatural which occurs when a sincere apology is offered. Where there is attack and defense, defense and attack, there is really no room for God to enter and to move redemptively.

The apology will break the stalemate in the cold war and open the avenue for summit meetings in which points of continuing conflict can be resolved. Many a deadlock in negotiations has been broken by a sudden change of heart on the part of one who, with repentance, said, "I am so sorry. Will you please forgive me?"

THE DESIGN OF AN APOLOGY

As I prepared my apology to Barbara I was as meticulous as I would have been in preparing a sermon. Little did I realize that it would yield more spiritual dividends than most any sermon I had ever preached!

Most apologies are forced and made from the platform of conflict. Generally it involves a harsh, gruff, "Well, I'm sorry!"—which, being interpreted, means, "I am sorry that we are having this trouble!" This type of apology is begrudgingly given and even more begrudgingly received.

ON MAKING AN APOLOGY

1. Never make an apology in anger. This belies the very spirit of an apology and evidences no change in your attitude.

2. An apology for the sole purpose of calming the offended person is seldom genuine. Often, when a wife becomes upset, the husband, willing to do anything at any price, uses the tool

of an apology to calm her down. Such an apology is generally made sarcastically or condescendingly and later comes off as more of an insult than an entreaty.

3. An apology should be made from the platform of genuine conviction and evidenced with a measure of godly sorrow. It should be made seriously.

4. An apology should be made so as to avoid accusation. Never say, "Well, I'm sorry for what I did, but you ...!" A genuine apology has all fingers and thumbs pointing inward. This is no time for discussing her shortcomings, husband! You are the one making the apology and the principal subject is you! The attempt of justification is one of the first signs of an insincere apology.

5. Be honest and thorough in making an apology. Most husbands don't realize why wives need full information for security. The wife needs not only to see a genuine repentance in her husband who has not met her needs, but she needs to know that he realizes the full nature of his failure, and that it will not continue to happen. A wife won't put much stock in an apology which she has heard before and which was not accompanied by a change of attitude and behavior. When she hears the explanation of her husband's realization of his failure she is reassured. It is never enough for a husband to say to his wife, "I am sorry" or "I was wrong." She wants to know if you are aware just where you were wrong.

6. An apology is the time for the use of the first person pronoun, singular! This is not a time for "you" or even "we." In an apology "I" am the culprit.

7. Insist on finishing the apology before getting feedback from your wife. That will come more effectively later.

8. Reveal plans after the apology which give evidence to your wife that things are really going to be different. She will receive security from the fact that you have thought through

the situation. She will know that your apology is more than a design to calm the storm and to move on into another direction.

9. By making an apology you have assumed full responsibility for your marriage. You have acknowledged that anything out of line in your marriage is your responsibility. You may not be directly to blame, but you are directly responsible. You have acknowledged that your wife's conduct, appearance, and conversation are either your public condemnation or your public commendation.

10. When you have finished with the apology, leave it at that. This is not the time to extend the discussion in such a way as to leave her with the feeling, "Well, he just did that so he could get at me!" Neither should she feel that you expect her to make love to you merely because you have made this move. The fact that you do not expect lovemaking at that moment will confirm in her mind your sincerity.

11. Ask her to forgive you. Do not settle with anything but an outright answer. She may be prone to say, "I didn't take it this way; neither did I feel that you were so wrong." How wrong you were or were not is not her concern at this point. It was your business with God that caused the apology. Her business is to say, "Yes, I forgive you!"

Now, husband, because I am afraid that you may escape at this point, I am going to list some areas of failure with most husbands. I qualify as somewhat of an expert on this subject since thoughtlessness and insensitivity have been chiefest among my failures.

Not being aware of the wife's needs
Not being thoughtful
Paying attention to *someone* else (male or female)
Paying attention to *something* else (TV, football, golf, etc.)

Forgetting an important date, event, song, etc.
Not listening when she is speaking
Condemning or cutting her down in front of someone else
Failing to stand with her in conflicts with the children
Making plans without including her
Making purchases which should have included her consent
Fussing at her over spending
Walking out on an argument
Clamming up during an argument
Pouting
Criticizing her for criticizing others
Becoming defensive or angry when she wants to discuss matters
Failing to take the spiritual lead
Failing to grow in Christ
Not valuing her opinion or viewpoint
Rejecting her advice on the basis that she has no business sense
Manifesting impatience
Failing to confront her when needed
Unforgiveness
Selfishness in sex
Childish response when rejected
Failing to tell her "I love you"
Not expressing gratitude for her work in the home
Not complimenting her cooking
Not praising her good qualities
Not admitting your mistakes
Failing to do the little things that prove your love
Not being mannerly, waiting for her, opening car doors, etc.

I believe that most honest husbands can find some salient points in the aforementioned list. (Most dishonest husbands will have already quit us, anyway!)

HOW TO RECEIVE AN APOLOGY

The same afternoon the Lord taught me how to make an apology, he also taught me how to teach Barbara to receive one. So the same night I made the apology which changed the direction of our marriage, I taught her how to receive that apology. Here are a few points to remember.

1) Remember that any apology you as a wife receive as a result of your pressure, accusation, or demands is unlikely to be sincere and meaningful. "I demand an apology!" seldom elicits a sound and meaningful apology. Such an apology may satisfy your pride for a moment, but it will yield little fruit later.

2) Don't interrupt the apology by passing it off lightly. Never say such things as, "It was nothing!" It *was something!* Let him finish. Wait until you are asked to forgive to do so.

3) Don't agree with his confessions with your own embellishments. This is not the time to take advantage of his humility by further accusation. You will get much more mileage out of God's conviction than by your own accusations. An ounce of God's conviction is worth more than a ton of your accusations!

4) Do not penalize for the apology. In the apology, the husband is making himself more vulnerable than he ever has before. If he is attacked at the time of the apology, he is less apt to be inclined to apologize again. If something lingers in your mind save it until later.

5) This is no time to lecture. As your husband makes the apology leave him in charge of the conversation. This is his session. Let him conclude it as he wishes. Be supersensitive about what to do when he finishes.

6) When he asks for forgiveness, don't settle for a simple "yes." It is better to say something like, "Yes, I forgive you and appreciate more than I'll be able to tell your willingness to explain where you believe you've failed me."

7.) When you have forgiven, never take "parting shots." More than a few times couples have allegedly put their swords away and laid down their shields of defense, only for one or the other to make a quick draw of the sword and thrust the other through.

8.) Please realize that once forgiveness is granted with an act of the will, you forfeit forever the right to bring up in the future that which has been forgiven. We often use the term "forgive and forget." But technically to forgive and forget is an ability locked within the heart of God. He is the only One who can really forgive and forget. Our minds are so constructed that the more we try to forget a subject, the more we concentrate on it, and thus the better we remember it. The result is that, in trying to forget a thing, we add guilt to ourselves in the very attempt.

I have a better suggestion ... *forgive ... and remember the matter as forgiven.* Such a sanctified memory will produce more love, and will make more precious the relationship and more valid the continuing power of the blood of Jesus. To forgive means, in the language of the New Testament, "to bear away." There is in every heart a memory chamber for unpleasant memories. That is where bitterness is born if the place is often visited and memories remain there. This chamber should be cleaned out often.

You ask, "How can I get rid of an unpleasant memory?" The simple answer is, "Take the memory and make it a pleasant one." Remember that Samson one day met a lion in the road and there was an awful struggle. I imagine that, though the lion was killed, Samson was badly clawed. A bad memory! But a few days later he came back by and found honey in the carcass of that lion, enough for him and his family. So "out of the carcass came forth sweetness." That will happen to you.

9.) This may be the best time for you, wife, to say, "Well, dear, I haven't been without fault in this matter." If God has revealed some areas in the process where you ought to apologize, do so. If not, don't force it. It may be better, later.

10) What a time to respond with yourself and your availability! It will be much more valuable and meaningful to him since he has been instructed not to expect it. If there is any time when you are justified (and I think there is) in being aggressive in the physical relationship, that time is now! Such response is valuable in developing and maintaining a deep and transparent relationship. He will not soon forget the experience and will not be hesitant the next time an apology is needed.

THE DYNAMICS OF AN APOLOGY

There is nothing quite so powerful as a sincere apology. It opens the door for further communication and settles conflicts. It yields to the spirit of the cross and moves from retribution to redemption. It invites the Spirit of God into the arenas of men. It arouses admiration on the highest plane and secures a truce of the highest order. It adds depth to any relationship and blazes the trail for deeper fellowship in the future.

It encourages the deepest self-giving without fear of being hurt. Husband, please know that when your wife hears an apology from you, she will hear far more than you have spoken. She will likely hear the following, and more.

"I actually care and realize your needs."
"I am really going to be different."
"I love you more than I love myself."
"I commit myself to meet all your needs."
"I really want to be sensitive to you."
"I have plans for continuing improvement of our marriage."

The dynamics of apology are so extensive that perhaps the best has not been said. Better than the discussion is the experiencing of these dynamics. Let's move on!

PROJECT AT THE END OF THE CHAPTER

Husband, ask the Lord to reveal exactly where you are to start in making a sincere apology. Study it, prepare it, and make it, using the principles in this chapter. Discuss this chapter with your wife. Life's three hardest words, "I was wrong," may indeed lead to life's happiest wonders!

7
OUR DIFFERENCES...
DIVISIVE OR DYNAMIC?

DON'T FIGHT IT...FACE IT!

Male and female created he them (Genesis 1:27b).

"Most men cannot understand that women have problems men cannot understand! Men and women are different in many ways:

> They express themselves differently.
> They handle their feelings differently.
> They make decisions differently.
> They face other people's problems differently.
> They seek to change one another differently.
> They fight differently.
> They view the home differently.
> They view marriage differently.
> They express love and sex differently.
> They respond to sin and guilt differently.
> They view themselves differently and expect each other to respond differently."[1]

Let's face it, we're different! In fact, if we do not face it, it will be disastrous!

Let's face another fact—God made us to be different. God is a God of variety. He seems to disdain sameness and to avoid

stereotyping. The leaves on the trees vary. Human fingerprints
are all different. Every separate entity in God's creation has a
separate identity. This genius of variation is never more obvious than in the male-female consideration or in the marriage
relationship.

If the fact that I am not like you and you are not like me is
the basis of our conflict, then we are locked into a hopeless
struggle. For all of us are different and cannot be the same. If
we tried to make everyone the same, we would immediately
have two more problems.

First, there would be the problem of deciding precisely who
would be the norm. Would you be more like me or make me
more like you? Would men be like women or women be like
men?

Second, what would then be the purpose of life if everyone
were the same?

So men and women are _equal but not identical._ We always
have been and always will be equal. We have never been and
will never be identical. And yet, irony of ironies, do you realize
that millions of people are working themselves to death to
attain an equality they already have? And millions of others
are fighting over the fact that they are different and will never
be anything but different!

Yes, we are different and God wills it so. We are equal, too,
and God wills that. We can try to be the same but we never will
be. We can try not to be equal but we will always be.

There is a domestic evil under the sun, namely, married
couples in conflict seeming to have one deranged demand, "If
I am to love you, you must become like me." They seem to be
saying, "The reason I cannot love you is that you are not like
me."

The husband who is to live with his wife "according to
knowledge" must understand the basic differences in the male
and female mystiques. He must not make the common mis-

take of deriving what he *thinks he knows* about his wife from what *he knows* about himself. This will lead to a total breakdown in understanding. On the other hand, I know of nothing that will aid the marriage relationship more than understanding these basic differences.

I am going to deal with two major areas of differences in this chapter. First, I will treat those basic differences between the male and female mentality. Then we will discuss the variations in habit and temperament almost universal in husband and wife relationships.

COMPARING THE MALE AND FEMALE MENTALITY

In this discussion I am calling for an acceptance of the fact of variation. We must not hold each other responsible for the fact that we are different. This immediately reveals two flaws in the thinking. First, there is the fallacy of holding that another's condition, different from mine, is not valid. The second fallacy is the supposition that one could change his or her basic nature if he or she tried.

When Adam made his acceptance speech in Genesis 2:23-24, he doubtlessly recognized that the creature standing before him was drastically different in design from himself. And that was only the outside! Later he was surely to discover that the greatest differences between himself and her were not visible to the eye.

Can you imagine how Adam might have expressed himself had God given him a person just like himself? I think it would have sounded much more like "Yuk! Lord, that's absurd! We don't need another me!" And yet, as ludicrous as this seems, much human conflict rages around this very idea. Many a man or woman strives for years to recreate their respective mate into his or her image and when, at last, that seems to be achieved they hate the result. It is as if they are saying, "I hate you because you have allowed me to make you like me!"

So let's accept the *declaration* that we are different. Let's further accept the fact that we are different, not by a freak of chance or nature, but by *divine design*. Let's further accept the fact that these differences are not our disadvantages but our *dynamics*. Thus convinced, we'll cease our weary struggle of seeking to recreate our mates in our own image and accept their differences as our greatest assets!

Now view some of these differences. I am well aware that some will take me to task for these generalizations, but I'll stick by them. I also recognize that, to one degree or another, every person has a combination of characteristics considered male and female.

MAN IS AN INITIATOR...
WOMAN IS A RESPONDER

Let's understand at the outset that either man or woman may, in fact, often engage in what the other is best characterized by. By that I mean that simply because man is the initiator does not mean that a woman may not initiate. Along the same line, just because the woman is a responder does not mean that a man may not respond.

If we understand this basic difference and accept it, we will not expect our mates to be the same or be angry if they are not. Trouble comes when one characteristic prevails to the exclusion of the other.

But even greater trouble arises when the husband, who by the right of his role, has the responsibility of initiation and does not accept and fulfill it. Either the woman must take the initiative, which is not hers, which will create a multitude of problems, or become passive, not having an initiator. Either way, the marriage is in trouble.

The initiator and the responder are both valuable and needed. Both reach out for perfection. Remember that the distinctions are never classic. There is always a mixture, a blend of both. There is a different tendency in each, making for harmony and fulfillment. When the mixture is right the result is tremendous.

In order to begin discovering the proper blend, the husband must accept himself as an initiator and lovingly pursue his office. Basically, every man, even the most passive, has a desire to initiate.

Likewise, every woman, even the most aggressive, both desires to respond and to have a man who will initiate.

You can see what can happen when these powerful tendencies are out of kilter. You have the same type of potential in electricity. Touch the wrong wires together and you have an explosion. A domestic short-circuit occurs when these differences touch wrongly. A woman, though by nature a responder, may through aggression conquer the male in her life and cause him to cower, only to discover later that the female in her becomes angry and frustrated at what has happened. She neither likes herself for doing to him what she has done nor that he is for allowing her to do it! But if you remember my opening thesis, you will bear in mind that he, not she, is finally responsible. The husband may not be to blame that this has happened, but he is responsible.

So, husband, whether this vast potential is divisive or dynamic is up to you.

LOGICAL . . . EMOTIONAL

Husband: "Dear, what you're saying doesn't make sense!"
Wife: "That's not my field, honey—it's yours!"
Now, remember that this doesn't mean the husband can't be emotional or that the wife can't be logical. The above conversation, or at least one similar, occurs thousands of times a day across the world. A wife makes an emotional response. She literally leads with her emotions. When she shares her emo-

tional response with her husband, it is usually a plea for his logic to help her put it all together. If the husband misreads this he will often by harshness wound the spirit of the relationship. This will discourage the wife in future entreaties on the basis of her emotions. If the husband doesn't understand this basic difference he will always accuse his wife of either being unreasonable (at best) or stupid (at worst). If the wife doesn't understand this she will accuse her husband of being unfeelingly logical (at best) or icily loveless (at worst).

But what a marvelous balance when these two fit together ... his logic and her emotions. The husband who does not accept the fact of female intuition will suffer much because of this negligence. Through initiative he may bring to his wife's attention a business matter about which she has no logical understanding. She may say, "I just don't feel right about it." The husband may say, "Dear, you don't know anything about it. You don't have *sense* enough to feel!" But the fact is that she does not feel on the basis of logic! The wise husband is the one who will hear the cautions of his wife, even in areas where she has no conscious knowledge.

I once made an investment (one of those *sure deals*) of money, which I couldn't afford, over the protests of Barbara. Oh, we discussed it, but she simply didn't know anything about it. Within weeks the whole scheme failed and we lost *every penny*. Though she didn't know anything about it, she was right! How did she know? God only knows! Husband—some wise advice: *when she talks, you listen!*

Here is the awesome dynamic of this variation. The husband, being logical and accepting his wife as emotional, brings up a matter to his wife for her confirmation or disapproval. He will accept with dignity the value of her response. Both are winners. A right decision is made and mutual respect has increased.

A wife, being emotional and accepting the fact that her husband is logical, brings up a matter to her husband for the input of logic. He responds lovingly and logically, and she accepts the validity of his response. The result is both warmth and wisdom—mighty dynamics!

DOER . . . BE-ER

Man is an active creature and finds his satisfaction in exploring, experimenting, reaching out, and driving on. Woman finds her fulfillment, for the most part, in being. It is this combination properly accepted and practiced that helps build character in each other, as well as the children. The man finds his greatest fulfillment in doing his work. The woman who is able to bear children probably finds hers in being mother to those children. The nature of man's pursuits dictates that he will most always see the clear results of his success rather immediately. The wife's investments are more long-term and may not be as readily evaluated. For this reason the loving and thoughtful husband will make up the difference and give her his evaluation constantly in praise and thanksgiving.

THINKER . . . TALKER

A husband is often lost in thought. His wife is often lost in talk! They need to find each other. She needs to rescue him before he drowns in his sea of thought. He needs to rescue her before she is blown away in a hurricane of words.

The thinker should talk, and the talker should think. Just as harmful as speechless thought can be to a marriage, so can thoughtless speech. But both together make for the kind of communication that liberates and promotes understanding.

The wise husband will become a talking thinker and will lead his wife to become a thinking talker!

There are many other natural variations. Some of these will be discussed more fully in the chapter on communication. Others will be discussed when we come to view our needs as husbands and wives. Let's look at a few of these.

A man looks for success, a woman, for security. Thus the man will find an extension of himself in his work. His wife will find the children, the home, and her ministry to him a fulfilling extension of herself. This causes them to view the home and its purposes differently. The man views the home as a place of rest and refreshment, a sort of a haven in the storm. A woman views the home much the same way as a man his work, an extension of herself. When the husband has no concern for repairing broken things in the house, the wife may read rejection into this since she identifies the house as an extension of herself. If the house is cluttered, she feels cluttered. She is sensitive when something is wrong in the home. A part of her is not right. For this reason the husband must develop some sensitivity in this area and respond quickly to suggestions for repair, rearrangement, or replacement of what is wrong.

A man, being logical and active, will often be insensitive or thoughtless, seeming preoccupied. A wife generally is both sensitive and thoughtful by nature since, being emotional, she knows the value of ministering to feelings. This will be reflected in the fact that a man will tend to deal with problems from the standpoint of solutions, while the woman will deal subjectively with the people within the problems. Women understand people with problems. Men solve problems for people. If men and women do not understand these basic differences, there will be mutual irritation and conflict. The man will be irritated that the woman cannot seem to remain objective, and the woman will be irritated that the man cannot seem to have deep feelings for the people involved. The fact is that both approaches are needed. Man needs a woman's sensitivity and woman needs a man's objectivity.

Men and women engage in conflict differently. Men are prone to use logic in conflict. Women fight from the trench of emotions generally. A man may use hard, intellectual logic, harsh words, or silence. He may desire to resolve the situation by forgetting it. Women, on the other hand, tend to react in a struggle by crying or even screaming or making a sweeping declaration sometimes with "You never ..." or "You always...."!

One man said, "When we get into a fight, my wife always gets historical." His friend said, "You mean hysterical, don't you?" "No," said the husband, "she gets historical, bringing up everything from the past."

The differences we have observed thus far in this chapter are those relating to natural variations in the male and female. Now let's look into the areas of temperament, unrelated to male-female differences.

I am certain that God has a sense of humor! One of the clearest proofs is found in the number of weird combinations God puts together in marriage. Have you ever noticed? Let's observe:

DIFFERENCES IN TEMPERAMENT

Mr. Deliberate and Mrs. "J. P." (for Jet-propelled!)

This happens too often to be coincidental! Here is a man who is the epitome of passivity. God chooses to put him with a woman who has one gear in her transmission ... *High Speed ... Forward!*

First, there should be praise that they are not the same. If both were like him, they would never get together. If both were like her there would be a chain-reaction explosion.

In this combination, then, she is provided direction by his deliberateness, and he is provided impetus by her impetuosity! This is not a drain but a dynamic. The key, as in all of these, is each accepting the uniqueness of the other's contribution with thanksgiving and love.

Mr. Punctuality and Mrs. "A. L." (for Always Late!)

Have you noticed how often God puts a man who is a stickler for time with a woman who seems to be habituated to lateness? If it is true that marriage (among other things) is God's celestial "frameup" to make both parties like Jesus as rapidly as possible, then we need to observe these differences closely. Why such a combination as the above? In all probability Mr. "P." has a patience problem as clearly as Mrs. "A. L." has a timing problem. Just what if her lateness, properly accepted, were to affect his impatience? Let me speak to that situation with a theoretical drama.

Mr. "P." is ready, as always, at least fifteen minutes before it's time to go. Mrs. "A. L." is not! She never is. He says that she never will be! But stay tuned.

Mr. "P." sits down and engages in his usual pastime while waiting for her—enjoying the rapid acceleration of adrenal fluids and thus working into a sort of a slow-burning rage. But he catches himself and begins to think. He loves his wife and knows (or at least, thinks) that God has led them together. God knew what she was like when they came together. *Is it possible that God allowed her to bring this 'lateness' into our marriage just to improve my life at the point of patience?* he asks himself. He continues, *Come to think about it, I love that woman so much, I'd rather have her thirty minutes late than anyone else I can think of on time!*

Mr. "P." then begins to praise the Lord for his "late" wife. He catches up on his Bible memory. He balances the checkbook and catches up on his magazine reading while he waits for her. When she appears (finally) he is delighted.

He stands up and gives her his arm. With measured caution Mrs. "A. L." takes it, and out they go to the car. He opens the car door on her side (of all things) and allows her to climb in. He gently closes the door when she is in. (Before, if he has opened her door at all, he has closed it with a slam that could have broken her foot!) She waits for the usual barrage which generally begins with the subtle reminder, "You're late again!" (Spoken in High A Flat!) But the barrage does not come. Instead a quiet, gentle, tender voice. She has to look to be sure that she has not gotten into the car with a stranger.

But it is he, saying, "Honey, you look terrific! I sure want to thank you!" She, firmly fixed at the armrest on her side of the car, replies, "You want to ... what?"

"I just want to thank you for being you and for being my wife. You know, all these years I've been complaining at your lateness. Tonight while I was waiting on you I just thanked God for your lateness—and all. I need a fresh batch of patience anyway, and nobody else in the world can help me with that like you! I just wanted to thank you. Your lateness helps my patience, and besides all that I had some time to catch up on some things while I was waiting on you!"

Fellow husband, you can almost be certain that she will be on time the next time! She will want to find out what you were doing while you were waiting for her!

Besides that, God is now free to deliver her from her problem of lateness since her problem of lateness has been used by God's design to deliver you from your problem of impatience.

If you do not see that principle, let's try again.

Mr. Silence and Mrs. "A. T." (for Always Talking!)

More than a few times (and perhaps in your case) there is the case of the silent man and the talking wife. It was so in our marriage. I was one of those husbands who could have lived for forty years on a series of unintelligible grunts. I felt like I had fully explained a point when I had grunted about it twice. Often such a man of silence is drawn to fall in love with a woman who feels like time is wasted when the air is not filled with the sound of her voice speaking on any subject which happens to be handy.

That this can pose a problem is without argument. I am a man who loves silence. My idea of bliss is silence! But I fell in love with a woman who loves to talk. For the first few years of our marriage, I almost drove her crazy by my silence, and she almost drove me crazy with her talking.

One day we awakened to the fact that God knew about us and our characteristics when we came together. Since his providence is all-inclusive, as we claim it to be, then even our "bad points" could be used to minister to each other. What a revelation! I had no difficulty believing that all her good points (which were many) could be used of God to make me a better man and a better Christian. Now I saw that even (and perhaps especially) her bad points (which were few) could be used of God to minister in my life.

And do you know that I accepted her talkativeness as a gift from God? Ever since I have been learning how to be more personally communicative! What was divisive turned out to be dynamic!

Now that you are thinking about it, why should God deliver your wife from being late if her lateness has not been allowed to minister to your impatience? Why should God deliver her from being over-talkative when you have not been delivered from being a noncommunicative bore? Why should you be disagreeable about her being high-strung when you have become hopelessly passive?

Are you beginning to feel the potential excitement in the very qualities that have been sources of conflict? The very pet peeves that have sparked controversies and left smoking battlefields have a vast potential for good. The very foibles that have been divisive now form the dynamics for deep relationships—and just plain fun.

No two people on the face of the earth are more different in their basic temperaments and personalities than are Barbara and I. She is vocal and high-strung. I am the silent type and extremely slow and deliberate. She is a planner. Administration is not my cup of tea. She is thoughtful and sensitive. I am like a bull in a china shop, forgetful and sometimes insensitive.

Now, if you don't think a combination like that, mixed with nonacceptance, will cause a perpetual explosion, you just haven't thought about it. But once we began to accept each other's differences, we began to find, to our utter delight, that these differences were our strongest advantages. The things that have been points of conflict have become points of growth.

I am now aware that the one person in all the world who possesses the grandest potential of ministering to my points good and bad, and to help usher me into Christlikeness, is none other than my wife. And I love her more at this moment than I ever have!

Please discover in your differences, your greatest dynamics!

PROJECTS IN DYNAMIC DIFFERENCES

1. Make a study of your last conflict with your wife. Did it center around anything you read in this chapter? What difference did it involve? Are you now conscious of a particular thing about your wife you would change if you could?

2. Observe the following list and mark by the side of descriptives "I" or "she" as to which one they best describe:

Noncommunicative	Moody	Talkative	Organized
Disorganized	Punctual	Often Late	Unfeeling
Carefree	Critical	Understanding	Gregarious
A loner	Unsure	Confident	Witty
Serious	Insecure	Needs approval	Lazy
Self-pitying	Diligent	Flexible	Disciplined

3. After marking these ponder them one by one for a few moments. Then ask: Am I as understanding with myself as I am with my wife? Do I condemn her for some things and condone things just as bad or worse in me? Maybe you need

to reread the apology chapter again—and then prepare one.

4. Have a praise time with the Lord for those differences in you and your wife, allowing Him to show you how dynamic these differences might be as you accept them.

5. As the time is ripe (and you will know) share your feelings with your wife and then listen to her as she responds.

8
OUR WONDERFUL PROBLEMS!

RIDE THE WILD HORSES!

Therefore I take pleasure in infirmities, in reproaches, in neces-sities, in persecutions, in distresses for Christ's sake: for when I am weak, then am I strong (2 Corinthians 12:10).

It is almost redundant to write that the path of married life is flanked on every side with problems. In fact, all of life is full of problems. The Christian life is not a detour *around* those problems! It is a pathway *through* and *beyond* them! The com-mitted Christian marriage does not have less problems than any other kind. The truth is that it may have more! The differ-ence is that biblical principles form a foundation upon which we can cope with those problems.

Better still, the Christian faith finds an avenue of making these problems vehicles of glory and thankfulness.

J. Wallace Hamilton wrote a book entitled, *Ride the Wild Horses.* The title itself suggested that human emotions and abilities were wild horses that should be ridden. Any other course of action will prove destructive. I suggest that the same is true with respect to the marriage relationship. There will be problems. A couple which does not have problems does not have a relationship. Any treatment of those problems which is an attempt to avoid or disregard them will prove less than helpful.

Paul, in 2 Corinthians 12, opens a chapter on his life to reveal that he was once faced with a terrible and painful problem. He prayed to the Lord about that problem repeatedly. Finally God responded with, "My grace is sufficient for thee, for my strength is made perfect in weakness." Then Paul, with no further pleading, declared, "Most gladly therefore will I rather glory in my infirmities, that the power of Christ may rest upon me. Therefore I take pleasure in infirmities, in reproaches, in persecutions, in necessities, in distresses for Christ's sake, for when I am weak, then I am strong" (2 Cor. 12:9-10).

Paul had learned to accept his problems and allow them to be the source of his strength. He had learned to ride the wild horses.

COUNT ME A CONVERT!

My policy was formerly to avoid conflict at any price. This is neither wise in business nor marriage. If there is conflict, it should be faced and expeditiously handled. It is not always the most peaceful approach. Fleeing has solved few problems. It merely relocates them, and usually the relocation provides a more fertile climate in which they can grow!

Barbara and I have had problems. I hope you and your wife have some! If you don't have some, allow Barbara and me to give you some of ours. As a husband, I must admit, I came late to see that all of our problems were my responsibility.

Barbara is a confronter. I am an avoider. In times past we have played the game—confront and avoid! She confronted ... I avoided! It happened quite by accident that day, at least from my standpoint. We had a point of conflict (which was not unusual). She confronted me (which was usual). I defended (which was usual). And so on. After a while I became so angry that I was consumed. I could do nothing but weep inside and was about to do it outside. I didn't want anyone to see a grown man cry, so I tried to keep it to myself. The problem was that I could not escape.

We were en route to the airport. I couldn't jump out of the car! Finally we arrived at the airport, and instead of the usual amenities I walked off to catch my plane. Needless to say, Barbara sensed that something was wrong. She followed me and asked me what was wrong, and, of all places for this momentous occasion, I chose the third largest airport in the world to tell my wife off!

I let loose. I blasted off like a rocket and twenty-five years of pent-up emotions came spilling out all over the airport. I wept, I moaned, I did all but curse (and came close to that)! I would have been mortified had a friend walked up about that time. I finally finished without missing my plane, and Barbara meekly and politely asked, "Well, do you want me to leave?" Now, I am not sure what she meant by that question, whether she meant leaving the airport, the house, the town, the nation, or the world. But I was sure about one deal. I had blown it! Now she saw me for what I really was and had been hiding from her all along! I think I said, "Frankly, I don't care!" (Not quite that nicely) And at that particular moment, I didn't. I suggested that she go home and sit down and think—just think!

Well, we parted with not too friendly a parting. Imagine me, going to minister spiritual life in a faraway state. I boarded the plane and prayed that no one would be in the next seat who needed to be witnessed to about Christ. I was in no state or mood to minister. I was physically sick. I asked the Lord to forgive me and he did. I asked Barbara to forgive me and she did. I asked me to forgive me, *and I didn't!* But when I arrived back home, my wife was sweeter and our relationship was better than it had ever been. We began to discuss our problems and came to realize that most of our discussion heretofore had been amid the problem when neither of us was in a condition to communicate constructively about it. After the problem we would forget about it—until the next time.

Allow me to speak about what Barbara and I have learned concerning our problems. They are like Hamilton's wild horses, and they had been stampeding for years, and we were caught in the stampede every time. We discovered that they could be ridden with delight. Observe the following suggestions:

ACCEPT THE FACT OF THE PROBLEM

You will never solve your problem by skirting it, denying it, avoiding it, or rationalizing it. Often the problem is not the problem at all. The real problem is made up of all the reactions that have been fed into the mind-computers of the husband and wife which come out on the printout during a confrontation. The problem never gets discussed. Tempers flare. Words fly. Battle-axes swing. The problem is unattended. The marriage is wounded by words that cannot be retracted.

> Boys flying kites can haul in their white-winged birds,
> You can't do that when you're flying words!

Husband, in the midst of it, admit that there is a problem. I have. I have not forgotten that I was telling you about Barbara and me. We accepted the fact that we had problems. It began to work miracles in our relationship! When we moved past the initial "shame" of having problems, we were then ready to deal constructively with them.

ACCEPT CONFLICT AS POTENTIALLY CREATIVE

I have hated conflict all my life. I will walk a mile around a conflict. My father was a stern disciplinarian, and I love him for that, but there were some times when I was involved in conflicts I would love to have avoided.

Barbara had been around conflict all her life. She was a product of a broken home. We came away from our family backgrounds with differing views of conflict. My view was, "Avoid it!" Hers was, "Accept it! Talk about it! Fight it through!"

"I will not fight with you!" I often asserted. She began to teach me that conflict could be creative, especially if it were harnessed in the framework of love and acceptance ... both of ourselves and of each other. It began to work. We began to listen to each other in conflict and heard some things we hadn't heard before. We learned some things about ourselves and each other that have been beneficial ever since.

ADOPT GROUND RULES
FOR CREATIVE CONFLICT

These can be agreed on with the knowledge that there will be conflicts in which to try them later on. Barbara and I discovered that most of our substantive discussions were carried on within the shadow of a great conflict. We realized that we seldom discussed problems unless we were in the throes of one at the time. We began to discuss our actions and reactions and why we felt that they existed. We became thoroughly honest with each other without feeling that we would be penalized. Some of those ground rules should be:

1) Avoid accusation by saying, "I feel ...," instead of saying, "You did this ... " (accusation). This leaves the other one space to explain his/her actions.

2) Avoid generalities such as "You always ... " or "You never.... " We noticed that Barbara would often say this and it would blow me away! When we investigated this we discovered that the statement left no further discussion. I had been a double-blank as a husband. Now, that was not what she meant, though it was what she said. So we agreed to remind

each other *never* to say *never or always* in such sweeping generalities. It has been a source of fun instead of frenzy ever since.

3) Use entreaty, not complaint, as the best approach. Entreaty assumes a kind response. Complaining predicts non-response and generally gets it!

4) Agree that each has the right to call off a discussion until a later time without being penalized.

5) Learn to read the stages of a conflict in order to avoid unnecessary complications through further accusations. There are times when it is best to shut up!

AFTER-THE-PROBLEM DISCUSSIONS ARE A NECESSITY

Barbara and I decided to have a three-day seminar, just she and I. We had hours of discussion, questions and answers, reports, and we took copious notes. We came out with several pages of typewritten notes. We then went back over what we had discussed. The results were electric! In a way I would love to be able to tell you that this took place way back in the sixties or at least ten years ago. It would make me feel less vulnerable in sharing it. But the fact is that it has taken place within recent months of this writing.

We couched our discussion within the context of the following outline. I will discuss parts of this more fully when we come to the all-important matter of communication.

HUSBAND-WIFE SEMINAR (JACK TAYLOR AND BARBARA TAYLOR)

1. *CHARACTER CHANGES WE WOULD LIKE TO EFFECT*
   JRT in JRT (What I would like to see changed in me)

BT in BT (What Barbara would like to see changed in her)
JRT in BT (What I would like to see changed in her)*
BT in JRT (What she would like to see changed in me)*
* Handle with care!
JRT and BT in the character of their marriage. (What we would like to see changed in our corporate relationship)

2. *GUIDELINES IN COMMUNICATION*
Under this we discussed "dos" and don'ts." This will be discussed more fully under the chapter title, "Let's Talk It Over.

3. *DANGER SIGNS IN COMMUNICATIONS* (Discussed later)

4. *CONFRONTATION IN RELATIONSHIPS* (Discussed later in chapter on Confrontation Therapy)

5. *CHARACTER TRAITS WHICH ARE REVEALED IN STRESS, FATIGUE, OR PRESSURE* (These were especially helpful as we admitted them and then discussed how to avoid them.) We used the model of the prodigal's older brother in Luke 15 as expressing feelings to watch out for in our own lives:
Anger (He was angry . . .)
Isolation (. . . and would not go in)
Self-pity (You never gave me a kid . . .)
Pride and defensiveness (I have never broken your commandment)
Accusation of brother (He has devoured his living with harlots)
Accusation of father (You never gave . . . you killed for him the fatted calf . . .)
Self-centeredness (Big "I" all through the dialogue)

A. What JRT sees in JRT (We found it more helpful to reserve these observations for ourselves. We would be harder on ourselves than the other would have!)
1. Disloyalty

    2. Impatience
    3. Independence
    4. Irresponsibility
    5. Laziness
    6. Unbelief
    7. Accusation
    8. Cowardice
    9. Refusing confrontation
   10. Self-condemnation
   11. Pessimism
   12. Negativism
   13. Close-mindedness
   14. Lack of love

(Note: I was first and led out. Would you have dared to believe that the author of this book was capable of all of these? He is and *so are you!* The sooner you admit it, the sooner you can trust the Lord for victory!

B. What BT sees in BT (The list was somewhat the same with a few exceptions involving personality variations.)

(YOU SEE, WE WERE ENGAGING IN VULNERABILITY EXERCISES WITHOUT FEAR OF INTIMIDATION OR CONDEMNATION. Don't you dare tell anyone about all our faults! These are secrets just for you readers!)

6. DIRECTIONS ON HOW TO EXPRESS FEELINGS OF FRUSTRATIONS, HURT, ANGER, AND DISAPPOINTMENT

(This is most helpful since both agreed that we would immediately put these into practice. If we forget and penalize each other, we simply refer to our notes!)

A. State the case without accusation, leaving a way open for apology, explanation, or defense.

B. Anticipate reception, approval, and success in statement of case.

C. State the case as positively as possible.
D. Ask for protection . . . making specific requests.
E. Engage in discussion of facets of the problem.
F. Make a mutual commitment to a program of improvement involving both of you.

Frankly, that was the most helpful husband-wife seminar I ever attended! Barbara heartily agrees!

Robert H. Schuller has a bully suggestion:

> Read this affirmation out loud, "I will be a different person when this problem is past. I will be a wiser, stronger, more patient person; or I will be sour, cynical, bitter, disillusioned, and angry. It all depends on what I do with this problem. Each problem can make me a better person or a worse person. It can bring me closer to God, or it can drive me away from God. It can build my faith, or it can shatter my faith. It all depends on my attitude. I intend to be a better person when this problem leaves me than I was when it met me."[1]

Charlie W. Shedd gives further light as he shares *Seven Rules for a Good Fight:*

1. Before we begin we must both agree that the time is right.
2. We will remember that our only aim is deeper understanding.
3. We will check our weapons often to be sure that they're not deadly.
4. We will lower our voices one notch instead of raising them two.
5. We will never quarrel or reveal private matters in public.
6. We will discuss an armistice when either of us calls "halt."
7. When we have come to terms, we will put it away till we both agree it needs more discussing.[2]

NOW, DO IT!
I believe that you have enough information to begin dealing

with your situation. Husband, remember, you are the initiator. It is in your hand. You are to lead the seminar. You are to be in charge of the discussion. Your wife will not resent that. She will bask in the glory of it!

Project on Problems:

1. Take one hour with your wife to discuss one of the five areas of the husband-wife seminar such as CHARACTER CHANGES WE WOULD LIKE TO AFFECT. You take the lead in sharing areas in your life that you would like to see changed. Listen to your wife.

2. Discuss awareness projects relating to these character traits and adopt a system of monitoring each other.

3. Begin to discuss plans for a longer time alone, perhaps out of town when you can go more deeply into the whole seminar material. Further suggestions for planning this will be made later.

9
CONFRONTATION THERAPY

SPEAKING THE TRUTH IN LOVE

But speaking the truth in love, may grow up into him in all things, which is the head, even Christ (Ephesians 4:15).

Though we have dealt in a measure with confrontation in the previous two chapters, now I want to speak more definitely about procedures in confrontation.

In his marvelous little volume, *Caring Enough to Confront*, David Augsburger writes, "Care-fronting is the key to effective relationships. It's the way to communicate with truth and love. Speaking the truth in love is the way to the mature right relationships shown to us in Jesus. 'Truthing-it-in-love,' the original phrase Paul chose, sums up the care-fronting way of responding and respecting each other by taking the Jesus way through the conflict.

"Care-fronting has a unique view of conflict. Conflict is natural, normal, neutral, and sometimes even delightful. It can turn into painful or disastrous ends, but it doesn't need to. Conflict is neither good nor bad, right nor wrong. Conflict simply is. How we view, approach and work through our differences does, to a large extent, determine our whole life pattern."[1]

Augsburger further suggests that there are five basic alternatives open in most conflict situations:

1. "I'll get you!"
2. "I'll get out."
3. "I'll give in."
4. "I'll meet you half way."
5. "I care enough to confront."[2]

All of us are dealing with conflict in one of these ways. We may decide on revenge (1), escape (2), defeat (3), compromise (4) or confrontation (5). Augsburger suggests, and I agree, that only through confrontation is there a creative outlet through conflict.

For our brief discussion in this chapter I want merely to suggest procedures and rules in confrontation therapy. We will observe suggestions under two headings, Administering Confrontation and Accepting Confrontation.

ADMINISTERING CONFRONTATION—

The Sooner the Better in Most Cases

Most cases of conflict worsen with waiting. This is perhaps accentuated in the marriage relationship. The couple lives in the same household and every exposure without clear communication simply serves to heighten (or deepen) the conflict. The best rule is generally "as soon as we are alone together" and "as soon as I can speak the truth in love."

Not In Anger

It should be done firmly but without anger. Waiting too long intensifies the danger of anger. Time gives space to imagine reactions and to fantasize our responses.

Be Positive—Assume a Total Response—Expect the Affirmative

This is not an attack with destruction in mind. It is an entreaty with purpose. The tone of the voice, the set of the face, the look in the eyes are all a part of the entreaty.

Don't Criticize or Condemn

This causes paralyzing defensiveness and encourages retaliation.

Map Out a Course of Action

Once the problem is pointed out, a positive course of action for the future should be plotted. Full success should be anticipated in this endeavor. It will involve both of you. As the husband makes a confrontation (and it can work both ways) he should acknowledge that any problem his wife has is his problem, too. We are not really talking about "your problem" but "our problem."

There Should Be an Openness to Question Without Intimidation

The question is always better than an outright statement when there is not the absolute certainty existent. "You broke our agreement!" would not be as well-received as a question, "What did we agree on that we would do in cases like this?" No defense is necessary here—just an answer.

Work Out Terms or Signs Which Humorously Remind Each Other of Past Conversations

"Never say 'never' " has been used dozens of times since the day we agreed that "never" should *never* be used in accusation. It has always been enjoyable and communicative. Our notes have served us well to remind each other of lines, quips, or funny stories. Barbara and I have identified ourselves with animals whose dispositions correspond with ours. She is a "skunk," and I am a "turtle." We have agreed that when in doubt, she "sprays." My "turtle" complex often needs attention. When trouble comes I tend to pull my head in and wait until the storm passes. Subtle reminders of these things on the part of either generally arouses the needed memory patterns. Laughter can often serve to ease tension and open up further communication.

As Husband Affirm Your Wife with Love and Blessing

There is all of that childlike desire to be directed in the right manner. It was comforting when my father corrected and directed me. I find security in it to this day. A wife appreciates a husband who will remind her of needs in her life and give attention to meeting them.

Tim Timmons defines a blessing as "calling favor down upon."[3] One can bestow a blessing when he holds no offense, desires to return good, and is willing to commit the situation with everyone involved to the Lord.

Make An All-Out Commitment to a Program of Victory Together

Remember that there is no failure as long as we are together. We have the presence and power of the Spirit of God upon our endeavors.

RECEIVING CONFRONTATION

Be Still and Listen Respectively

Trust your mate that he or she will be fair. If not, that is God's problem, anyway.

Take Notes for Relevant Reply and Future References

This will exhibit a listening disposition, preparing the situation for maximum communication.

Learn the Art of Entreaty

The *how not* and the *how to* of entreaty are demonstrated in the story of the older brother in Luke 15. The older brother precipitated a confrontation by:

Getting angry
Sounding off in his anger
Accusing everyone who got in his way
Defending present actions by past behavior
Attacking the actions of the father

But his father replied in a manner which demonstrates how to make a godly entreaty. He consummated the confrontation by:

Not reacting to the son's anger
Pointing to past fruitful relationships
Reminding of conditions which could cause common joy

Often a frantic and unpleasant confrontation can be turned around by a wise entreaty.

Ask for Advice

"I know that I have this problem and I want help in it. Tell me how I can think in my mind so I can avoid it."

"Let me tell you how I think this misunderstanding occurred so you can tell me where my thinking went astray."

Submit to Plans for Victory

A wise husband will have suggested a wise plan for future prevailing. A wife's vocal submission to those plans will enlist his full support in subsequent situations.

Leave Communication Lines Open with Gratitude

"I want you to know that I appreciate your bringing up this matter, and I want you to do it every time."

"I appreciate more than I could ever tell you your willingness to become vulnerable to share this with me. I know you love me and this causes me to love you even more."

Such interaction sets the stage for more transparent relationships.

EXAMPLE OF A CONFRONTATION:

Husband: "Honey, may I share something with you?"
Wife: "Yes, what is it?"
Husband: "I really feel that you're too vocal about the situation that came up at the party last night."
Wife: "Oh, really? I hadn't thought of it. What did I say?"
Husband: "Well, you made a judgmental statement about Mr. _____. You said he was a racist."
Wife: "Did I say that? I think he is, but I didn't intend to say it. But I often say what I'm thinking without noticing it."
Husband: "Do you remember our discussion when we promised that we'd allow the Lord to set a guard at the door of our lips and we promised that we'd help each other, too?"
Wife: "Yes, I sure do, and I appreciate your calling it to my attention. Darling, what can I do to guard against this happening next time?"
Husband: "Well, the Bible says to be slow to speak and slow to wrath. I believe that if you'll be quick to hear and slow to speak, it'll help. In fact, I'm trying to learn that the world can do without my observations on most matters. I'll pray for you, and you can pray for me."
Wife: "Right! I promise to be more mindful of talking about people, and I'll speak the truth in love when the truth *needs* to be spoken. Thanks for bringing this up."

Admittedly not all confrontations will come out that smoothly, but I want you to get an idea of what a confrontation is.

10
LET'S TALK IT OVER

COMMUNICATE OR DISINTEGRATE

That the communication of your faith may become effectual by the acknowledging of every good thing that is in you in Christ Jesus" (Philemon 6).

The consensus among marriage counselors is that poor communication is the number-one problem in marriage. Without a doubt the most repeated complaint of wives is, "My husband never talks with me!" Men by nature are normally poor communicators on a one-to-one basis, even those who communicate with thousands by other media.

Communication is not the most important thing ... it is the only thing! Without it there is no relationship. As in no other area of the marriage relationship the husband must take deliberate steps to develop communication with his wife. And no area will yield more immediate and life-changing results when attention is given to it.

Husband, this is probably the most pivotal chapter of this book. Read it carefully. Begin talking with *yourself* about the real status of communication in your marriage. Ask your wife to tell you honestly if there is sufficient communication in your relationship with her. Yes, this is going to take some of your time! Communication demands that two people give each other their time and presence.

Nothing in our lives has yielded more dividends than the time we have deliberately set aside to communicate. The most valuable lesson I have discovered in many years is that a wife considers *any* communication better than no communication at all. Now that I think of it, I believe that Barbara and I learned this together. It mystified me that Barbara would seem to push for communication, even if she had to make me angry to do it. Then, when I would respond in anger at first, the whole spirit of our conversation would change. She seemed to delight in it. She would rather have me talking to her angrily than not talking to her at all!

Listen to one passive husband's plea. "Something must be done about women. My wife is always pushing my buttons, just to get a response. I don't think she cares about what kind of response she gets, just as long as I react. She pushed so hard the other day that I finally yelled at her and told her to lay off. She grinned as though I had given her a bouquet of flowers. She said, 'Usually I get no feeling out of you. I'd rather you yelled at me than to have you just sit there.' "[1]

Communication lies at the heart of a woman's needs. Through it most of her needs are met. She needs to be loved and have continued evidences that validate her feelings. The woman who does not communicate will suffer death in a part of her being where life's deepest responses are born.

These words can be posted on the door of any house, whether it is the house of government or the house of business—but more especially over your dwelling and mine—COMMUNICATE OR DISINTEGRATE!

DEFINING COMMUNICATION

When we consider communication, we normally think of words, but in reality words are only a small part of communication.

After years of research in the area of communication Albert Mehrabian suggests the following breakdown in the relationship of words to communication:

Words alone 7%
Tone and voice inflection 38%
Facial expressions, posture, and gestures 55%

The dictionary definition of communication is "to make another or others partakers of; give a share of; make known; recount."[2]

David W. Augsburger defines communication as "the meeting of meaning." He writes, "When your meaning meets my meaning across the bridge of words, tones, deeds, acts, when understanding occurs, then we have communicated."[3]

Communication, then, is the visual or vocal transmission of meanings from one to another or others.

A COMMUNICATION BREAKTHROUGH

I have waited until now to share one of the greatest communication breakthroughs in our marriage. Back in the days when I heard Barbara say, "I hear what you're saying," I did something that I had never done before. I asked, "What did you hear me saying?" She then proceeded to tell me some things that I had never really said. In fact, I had never even thought of the things she "had heard me say."

I asked her, "Where did you get those ideas?"

She replied, "I heard you say them!"

"Impossible!" I retorted.

Well, she insisted that she had heard them. We stopped and began to investigate this phenomenon. Had she been hearing phantom voices? Was I talking in my sleep? Was it all in her imagination? None of those!

What we discovered was this: we are emitting and receiving

communication all the time, only a part of which is vocal. A woman generally says more than she means. Much of the time she has to in order to get her husband's attention! But by natural order she is given to embellishing, magnifying, and describing through the view of her emotions. A man probably more often says what he means. He doesn't bother to embellish or proliferate his descriptions. And these two creatures must get together for communication!

The wife says more than she means, and the husband hears it. Since he knows about himself and not about her, he thinks to himself, *Since, when I speak, I say what I mean, she must mean everything she says.* This causes him to speak harshly, not responding to deep inner need. He doesn't say much, but he means what he says. The wife hears what he says but thinks, *Since I mean more than I say, I'll bet he's not saying all he means.* Since she has not heard him say much, she fills in the gaps with information that is, at the time, as valid to her as words (if not more). So she falls back on the total record of her husband in the past—deeds, looks, negligences, forgotten dates, broken promises, ad nauseam. It is all received as what he has said, whether or not he has said it. The fact is that she has heard him say something through all these things that are louder than the human voice can speak. As she responds now she forgets (and it is not really important to her) whether she *heard* him say it or *saw* him say it.

Barbara and I had solved the mystery of the unspoken words that she had heard! You see, she had heard them in the area where they count. I had spoken them, not with my speaking apparatus, but with my life. She had heard everything I had "said."

It is not the lack of communication that is the problem in marriage, for there is communication all the time. Communication is not something that you turn on and off like the radio or something that you pick up and lay down like the telephone. We are communicating all the time. In fact, we *are* communication.

DEVELOPING AN ATMOSPHERE
OF COMMUNICATION

Love is something you are and do before it is something you say. While it is important to let your wife often hear the words "I love you," it is equally important that an atmosphere be present where that statement can be believable.

Husband, you can be sure that your wife will hear much more than your words when you say, "I love you." If you haven't demonstrated your willingness to spend quality time with her, she will hear you say, "I love you, BUT ... I don't have time to spend with you. Other things and other persons are more important." I know you never said that in her hearing, but you said it in your being and doing. Let me make the following suggestions for developing an atmosphere conducive to good communication:

1. Check your own communication level with yourself. Do you practice honesty with yourself? Do you face situations or disregard them?
2. Check your communication level in places other than at home. Do you communicate well with your friends? Do you communicate well with your superiors, those under you, with strangers calling on you?
3. Evaluate your communication level with your wife and children. Enlist their help in that evaluation.
4. Make a total commitment to lead out in communication at your home.
5. Set aside time to communicate with your wife and family.

6. Preside over your home with love which dictates that truth be spoken in love. Disallow unkind remarks, criticism, helping all involved to rid your home of things which form obstacles to communication.

7. Check on all problem areas in the matter of communication and devise ways to solve them. Some of these might be:

Television   Dad's job   Athletic events
Attitudes of independence   No time

8. Ask God to create a spiritual atmosphere in your home and in every relationship there.

9. Discover the communication that comes through prayer and worship.

A plaque hangs at a prominent place in our home, reminding us of the constant need of communication:

I KNOW YOU BELIEVE YOU UNDERSTAND WHAT YOU THINK I SAID ... BUT I AM NOT SURE THAT YOU REALIZE THAT WHAT YOU THINK YOU HEARD IS NOT WHAT I MEANT!

GUIDELINES IN MARITAL COMMUNICATION

As Barbara and I came together to discuss the matter of communication we agreed on the following DOS, DON'TS, AND DANGER SIGNS:

DOS IN COMMUNICATION

1. Allow for temperament and gifts differences in your mate.
2. Build up a knowledge of your mate's sensitive areas.
3. Continuously confirm commitment to your mate.
4. Study how to express feelings. Remember there are several factors to remember in the use of words.

A. What you mean to say.
B. What you actually say.
C. What your mate hears when you speak.
D. What your mate thinks he or she hears.
E. What your mate says about what is heard.
F. What you think your mate said about what you said.

5. Defer to one another.
6. Ask questions, using inquiry without intimidation.
7. Comfort one another.
8. Build up one another with compliments.

DON'TS IN COMMUNICATION

1. Never say "Never...." This disregards all attempts as failures.
2. Never say "Always...." Same as above.
3. Never make direct accusations acting as judge, jury, and executioner.
4. Never take unfair advantage of a failure. That's no time for preaching.
5. Never take advantage of an apology.
6. Never withdraw your spirit.
7. Never walk out ... cutting off conversation.
8. Never bring up the past without mutual consent, and that for building, not accusing.
9. Never react in anger, impatience, or rejection.
10. Never condemn self as a ploy to make your mate feel guilty.

DANGER SIGNS IN COMMUNICATION

1. Feelings of suspicion
2. Over-talkativeness
3. Not listening (close-mindedness)
4. Negativism

5. Anger
6. Fatigue
7. Harshness
8. Impatience
9. Overbearing attitude
10. Rebellion
11. Bad attitude
12. Resentment and bitterness
13. Manipulation . . . trying to control mate

PROJECTS IN COMMUNICATION

1. Check the level of your communication. (You on left and your wife on the right)
   _____ communication excellent   _____
   _____ communication good   _____
   _____ communication poor   _____
2. List two things you feel you can do to improve the communications in your marriage.
   A. I will
   B. I will
3. Begin to set aside an hour each week to communicate. At first it will seem awkard but later will be enjoyable.
4. Discuss the last misunderstanding you had with your wife, communicating such things as:
   A. How did the misunderstanding occur?
   B. Where did we begin to deal with personalities and not issues?
   C. How did we resolve it?
   D. What can we do next time to avoid misunderstanding?
   E. What did we learn about ourselves during and after it?
5. Write your wife a letter sharing with her just why you love her and cherish her.

6. Read the following poem and determine to put it into practice each day for the following week. (At least once a day)

> Amid the cares of married life,
> In spite of toil and business strife,
> If you value your sweet wife,
>   TELL HER SO!
>
> There was a time you thought it bliss
> To get the favor of a kiss;
> A dozen now won't come amiss . . .
>   TELL HER SO!
>
> Don't act as if she's passed her prime,
> As though to please her were a crime . .
> If e'er you loved her, now's the time,
>   TELL HER SO!
>
> You are hers and hers alone;
> Well, you know she's all you own;
> Don't wait to carve it on a stone . . .
>   TELL HER SO!
>
> Never let your heart grow cold;
> Richer beauties will unfold.
> She is worth her weight in gold;
>   TELL HER SO!

11
A WIFE'S SPECIAL NEEDS

LOVE HER ... LOVE HER NEEDS

And the rib, which the Lord God had taken from man, made he a woman, AND BROUGHT HER TO MAN (Genesis 2:22).

Woman had her beginning with man and would always be associated with man. The fact that God, after having put the finishing touches on his female creation, brought her to man was indicative of the fact that upon man would devolve the responsibility of caring for her. He would meet her needs. They would meet each other's needs.

Those needs were to become tremendously complicated upon the coming of sin into the world through man. Her sorrow and pain would be greatly multiplied. There would be constant conflict between her offspring and the devil. Her desire would be to her husband, and he would rule over her.

HUSBAND, YOUR WIFE NEEDS YOU!

In the chapter we are going to look at a wife's special needs. We will later cover how a husband can meet those needs. We will discover that, among the needs of a husband, is that of meeting his wife's needs. A husband who is not meeting his wife's needs is haunted by failure. He may respond to that by immersing himself deeper into his business or taking time to learn about and meet his wife's needs.

Whatever we discover about the needs of a wife, we must remember that needs exist to be met. In the providence of God your wife was allowed to give your marriage those qualities which above all others would serve to bring out the best in you. We have already seen how her special characteristics, especially those a husband would like to change, have been allowed to perfect the husband. Not only does that special quality thrust the husband upon the grace of God, but it is in itself a clue about what God plans to do through the husband in the life of his wife.

We will discuss many needs in the wife's life from several points of view. In the final analysis, we will discover that what a wife really needs is her husband—available and caring! She was made with needs only he could meet. Her needs were proliferated and complicated by the fall. Her desires were to be toward her husband, and she was to be under his rule. This was not a punitive measure as much as it was the plan of progress in the divine purpose for man.

Husband, you are responsible for meeting your wife's needs. You are capable of meeting your wife's needs. In meeting her needs you are going to find your own needs met. Living with her according to knowledge will mean that you are aware of her special needs and sensitive to your responsibility.

Before we look at the needs of wives, it would be a good idea to remind ourselves that, while there are many needs common to wives, this does not say it all. A husband may be aware of all these needs mentioned in this chapter and still not be fully aware of all the needs of his wife. There is a danger in seeking to do what we are doing in this chapter. I fear that the impression may be left that every wife in the world has every need mentioned, and all the needs of all wives are covered in this list. Regardless of the thoroughness in covering the needs of wives, there will be some needs not mentioned. The reason is that every woman is an individual and has unique needs, relating to background, environment, education, and a myriad of other influences. She wants to be treated and understood as an individual, not as one among millions of women. Your wife is not just a woman among women. She is *your* woman, totally unique, desiring to be understood and loved. Meeting her needs will prove to be far more than knowing facts. It will involve knowing her intimately and understandingly.

Many of these items will fit your wife so well that you'll be suspicious that she had a part in writing this chapter. But, though there are problems and needs common to every wife, your wife will manage to have a few needs totally unique to her.

Another central fact is that your wife's needs may undergo change from time to time. You may wake up one morning and find a new need staring you in the face. Maybe a new era has come into the life of your wife—and your marriage. Your sensitivity during what she is passing through will be a safeguard against wounding the spirit of your marriage. The needs of a wife before the children come are somewhat different than they are after children. When all the children are gone, needs present themselves in a different fashion. Though some problems common to all wives will be present in every age of life, a wise husband will be watching with a sensitive heart for the special needs of his own wife to surface.

OBSERVING YOUR WIFE'S NEEDS

As I began to write this chapter I noticed that there are many statements about what the needs of wives were. I agreed with all of them. There was some overlapping but all seemed necessary. I want to list those for you to think about, and then share with you how I arrived at the final list of the chapter.

BILL GOTHARD ... ADVANCED INSTITUTE OF BASIC YOUTH CONFLICTS

1. A wife needs the stability and direction of a spiritual leader.
2. A wife needs to know that she is meeting vital needs in the life of her husband that no other woman can meet.
3. A wife needs to know that her husband cherishes and delights in her as a person.
4. A wife needs to know that her husband understands her and protects her in areas of her limitation.
5. A wife needs to know that her husband enjoys setting aside quality time for her so they might have intimate conversation.
6. A wife needs to know that her husband is aware of her, even when his mind is on other matters.
7. A wife needs to know that her husband is making investments in her life that will expand and fulfil her world.[1]

BETTY COBLE

1. She needs to identify who she is and like herself.
2. She needs to decide what she wants out of marriage.
3. She needs to learn to communicate with her husband.
4. She needs to feel the love of her husband.
5. She needs to find fulfilment in her marriage.[2]

CECIL OSBORNE

1. A wife needs security. (More than financial but inner security which comes from a husband's trust, admiration, and a wife's sense of being needed.)
2. A wife needs love.
3. A wife needs understanding.
4. A wife needs acceptance.
5. A wife needs attention.[3]

GARY SMALLEY

1. A wife needs to feel that she is first place in her husband's life.
2. A wife needs to feel that her husband is willing to share an intimate moment of comfort without demanding explanation or giving lectures.
3. A wife's need for communication is constant.
4. A wife longs to be praised so she can feel valuable.
5. A wife wants to feel free to correct her husband without fear of retaliation or anger.
6. A wife needs to know that her husband will defend and protect her.
7. A wife wants to know that her opinion is so valuable that her husband will discuss decisions with her, evaluate her advice, and then act upon it.
8. A wife needs to share her life with her husband in every area . . . home, family, and outside interests.
9. A wife wants her husband to be the kind of man her son can follow and her daughter would want to marry.[4]

TRUMAN DOLLAR

(These are listed under the title Twelve Common Problems of Twentieth-century Women)
1. Frustration at the absence of spiritual leadership
2. Meaningless life
3. Uncontrollable insecurity
4. Feeling unloved
5. Belief that the husband takes the wife for granted
6. Absence of trust
7. Loneliness
8. Need of intimate conversation
9. Lack of total commitment from husband
10. Children left totally for the mother to discipline

11. Inability to control emotions, spending, and daily activities

12. Bitterness[5]

I found these lists to be both helpful and revealing. There seems to be no basic disagreement among the sources as to a wife's needs—just different perspectives.

As I thought further about the final list of needs, I left my typewriter and went upstairs to my "resident expert" on a wife's needs, Barbara. I asked her to help me on this chapter. Without divulging any information I had on hand, I asked her to share with me (and you) her ideas about the needs of a wife. The following is a result of that discussion:

1. *A wife needs acceptance.* She needs to feel that she has been valued and received as a person of worth to her husband. The need of acceptance is such that it requires continuous affirmation. Rejection or fear of rejection is a problem in a vast majority of people. The wife looks to her husband for acceptance.

2. *A wife needs assurance.* There needs to be constant visible and vocal reassurance made on the part of the husband. It is not that she has a bad memory, but that she has a continuing appetite for assurance.

3. *A wife needs identity.* She is continuously asking, "Who am I? Will someone please tell me who I am?" She wants her husband to tell her who she is. A wise husband will help his wife to identify herself as a child of God with a meaningful relationship with Him and then as his wife. Following that will be her responsibility with the children. Loss of identity is not an uncommon problem in the life of a wife. Often a sudden change of locations, surroundings, or events will cause an identity crisis. If a wife's life is isolated in bringing up the chil-dren and not identified with her husband and his desires and

needs, she will likely have an identity crisis when the children leave home.

4. *A wife needs support and backing from the husband.* She needs to feel that her husband is on her side, even when he does not agree with her ideas or conduct. It is shattering when a wife is caused to feel that her husband is not in her corner.

5. *A wife needs understanding.* Better still, she needs to feel understood. I asked my wife if a man had to know everything about a woman in order to have that understanding. In the discussion we agreed that, if a man gave himself to seeking to understand his wife, he would surely succeed in meeting her need at this point. What he lacked in information he would more than make up for it with an understanding manner and make her *feel* understood.

6. *A wife needs trust.* Nothing is more debilitating in a wife's mind than suspicion or distrust. In trusting her he is saying, "I look upon you as a trustworthy person."

7. *A wife needs the confidence of her husband.* While akin to trust, confidence involves more than trust. She feels that her value as a person is tied to what you think of her capability. Again there is a constant need for visualized and vocalized reassurance at this point.

8. *A wife needs the attentions of her husband.* She needs to feel that her husband is continuously mindful. This is the reason that gentlemanly behaviour is so important to a woman. She reads into every little action either positive or negative clues to the care of her husband.

9. *A wife needs the praises of her husband.* Vocal adoration is a constant need of the wife.

10. *A wife needs physical help from her husband.* A wife's mental-spiritual-physical make-up is so closely interrelated that a failure in any area will show in all areas. Doing the dishes for your wife or helping her with the housework will have interrelated effect. Running the vacuum cleaner may have as much

impact as the expert exposition of a Scripture passage.

11. *A wife needs rest and time off from responsibilities.* She has a total sense of responsibility which negates the possibility of her forsaking a job. She will drive herself to total exhaustion if not given room to rest. If her husband does not lead out in this, resentment and bitterness will often result. What a sad report on your relationship if your wife thinks of you as a slave-driver!

12. *A wife needs leadership.* She asks in dozens of ways to be led. If she is not led, then independence and frustration will result. Loving leadership is a constant need. The wife needs a sense of planning and direction about her life as a wife.

13. *A wife needs tender, loving care.* Among her many moods there will be times when nothing else will work. "Just hold me!" will often be her plea. The wise husband should need no further explanation for unconditional action.

14. *A wife needs her opinions and ideas to be heard.* If a wife feels that she is not listened to seriously by her husband she will sense rejection.

15. *A wife needs protection against tendencies in her life which might be harmful to her welfare.* She needs to be reminded of boundaries relating to physical strength, emotional health, and spiritual depth.

16. *A wife needs to be included in financial affairs with freedom to spend a part of the money as her own with limitations.*

17. *A wife needs thoughtfulness on the part of her husband.* She needs to know that her husband is thinking of her. She can only know this through visible or vocal reminders.

18. *A wife needs pretty things.* The aesthetic sense of a woman is an innate feminine gift from the heart of God. It would be a dull world without this need.

19. *A wife needs constant assurance that her husband is committed to her medical needs.*When she is ill, she needs his care, his sympathy, and his presence as at no other time. His going to the doctor with her is also an encouragement to her.

12
THE MAELSTROM OF THE MID-LIFE CRISIS

THE STERN STRESS OF MIDDLE PASSAGE

Greetings from the mid-life crisis! I've done everything I know to avoid it. I've categorically denied it. I've sought to be disciplined enough so I won't notice it. I've asked God to make me so spiritual that it wouldn't be there. I've tried to blame it on my wife's menopause. I've tried to steer around it by staying so busy I wouldn't have time for it. But despite it all, here I am, slap-dab in the middle of the stern stress of middle passage.

Yes, Virgil, there really is a mid-life crisis. Believe me, it's real!

Many years ago, when I was a young (oh, me!) preacher, an "old, old" preacher about twenty-five years my senior shared an observation with me. He talked with me about his awakening to the fact that some unwelcomed changes were taking place in his brain and body. He was in his late forties at the time.

These changes began to happen while he was away from home on a preaching engagement. One day he mentioned these feelings in his mind and body to a physician in the host church. With an understanding smile the doctor had responded with a brief discourse on the mid-life crisis, which can be as certainly anticipated as the female menopause. I had no idea why this older friend had shared this bit of information with me, but I will be eternally grateful he did. That brief conversation came back to me when I began to notice that strange things were happening in my world, externally and internally.

WHY THIS CHAPTER?

I must candidly confess that one of the reasons for this chapter is: I am right now experiencing some of the changes of the mid-life crisis. Frankly, I am not sure whether I am coming in or going through or coming out (I think that uncertainty is one of the signs!). But there are other reasons. I am convicted that an elementary understanding of the nature of the mid-life crisis will help us to be better husbands and save our wives from considerable unnecessary suffering. So I am going to deal, in a most elementary manner, with some of the features of the so-called mid-life crisis.

DEALING WITH A DEFINITION

Defining the mid-life crisis is much like trying to hold a bubble of quicksilver under your thumb. It is difficult to particularize or be absolute. Though there are many conditions common to all men in mid-life, no two sets of conditions are identical. They differ with personality, situation, profession, and environment. The perimeters of time are variable and vague. It is effected by disciplines, backgrounds, and geographical surroundings. But as difficult as it might be, let's set forth a workable definition.

Mid-life Crisis—That period of life in which a man begins to experience certain biological, emotional, and mental transitions which seem to demand a thorough re-evaluation of all facets of life

Someone described it properly when they referred to it as the "stern stress of middle passage." In this crisis time man reaches a state when life tends to be most prosaic. He seems to be too far from the morning to be romantic and too far from the evening to be softened by the thought of going home. He comes to the point when potatoes replace petunias in his garden of life. He seems to be in that time trap where he looks longingly at the youth he used to be and somewhat fearfully at the old man he suspicions he soon will be.

It is interesting that many doctors deny the existence, in fact, of the mid-life crisis. It is further interesting that most of these doctors are under forty years of age!

THE CULTURE CRUSH

Old age is not revered as it once was. White hair is not the crowning glory to our generation as it seemed to be in Bible days or in certain Oriental cultures today. At present "Grecian Formula" seems to be ahead in the polls.

Cultural patterns in the Western world are not kind to old age. It does offer mock kindnesses which appear to be benevolent to the aging. One nation in the Third-World bloc simply moves its aging citizens to dark, dingy houses on a downtown street to sit and await their demise. There is a superstition there which makes it unwise to have someone die in your residence. Hence, when it appears that death is imminent the aging person is simply moved from the residence where others live to a "death house" in the run-down area of the teaming city. In the West we have other, and not so crude, manners of dealing with age. While we in our Western culture have more good reasons to look forward to aging, there are other features which are counter-productive.

Our athletes, the folk heroes of our generation, are through between thirty-five and forty years of age. It is not uncommon to be a "has-been" at thirty-six!

Many businesses are looking for young executives. Young people seem to get ahead in shorter time than older people. In the ecclesiastical world churches are often looking for younger preachers (preferably under thirty-five with twenty-five years of experience!).

With old age many associate fears of uselessness, monotony, and loneliness. It is a fact of our culture that one of the stress points of the mid-life crisis is the fear associated with aging.

With our highly industrialized age there is a success syndrome which grips most men. Success at any price seems to be the goal of many men. The inevitable criteria of success involve properties, monies, and social and/or political clout. There comes a time in the lives of most men when they achieve a measure of all that they have equated with success. They immediately find that it does not yield the satisfaction anticipated during the search. There is then an expected crisis.

Another fact in our culture is the idea that man should be strong and fearless, always be in charge of the situation, and never mystified by problems. So, when he has a problem the man, in fact, has two problems. First, *he has a problem.* Second, *he is not supposed to have problems.* Couple these facts with the reality that a man is not inclined to vocalize his needs to anyone, and you have a man who is a prisoner within the walls of his own silence, suffering alone.

These and other facets of the contemporary cultural crush often drive a man to question whether or not he is successful in terms of the philosophies of his age.

THE BIOLOGICAL BIAS

It has been mentioned in varied articles and books on the mid-life crisis that certain chemical alterations and hormonal changes could be factors. There is some evidence that the amount of free testosterone (the male hormone) may change during the mid-life years. Free testosterone is that which is not tied to protein. However, there is simply not enough evidence to be conclusive. Other biological factors are more clearly suspect.

If you tend to suck in your beltline and stick out your chest as you walk in front of a mirror, you may be in the suburbs of the mid-life crisis. Certain biological changes are evident at this age. New pains, shorter breath, the necessity of more rest, and fatigue are some physical signs which appear. The mid-life man is generally finding a shift of his body weight toward the middle. He may frightfully notice a decrease in his sexual capacities. His whole body tends to experience a let-up.

We live in a generation of super athletes and are reminded of their feats and prowess several times a week. The idea that such abilities are equated with true masculinity is prevalent. We in the middle-age years are apt, because of this, to insist on staying with the church softball team longer than is advisable. We notice our muscles are losing their tone, regardless of how far we try to run or how much we try to exercise. It takes longer to get over severe exertion than before. Our stamina is just not what it used to be.

If in such a situation the mid-life man can't get his mind in gear with his body, he is apt to feel like a young man imprisoned in an old man's body. The results can range from amusing to annoying to near-tragic. Such a controversy between man and his body can lead to overreactions in dress, social behavior, and work habits. Flashy clothes, a new sports car, and more frequent flights to "funland" are a few of the possibilities.

Thus embroiled in such a struggle, the mid-life man may find his preoccupation disrupting his responsibilities as a husband and a father.

INITIAL EVIDENCES OF THE MID-LIFE CRISIS

I remind you again that there are no rules which are hard and fast when it comes to describing the mid-life crisis. There are, however, certain evidences which may suggest that the crisis is near or upon us. Let's observe a few of them here.

RE-EVALUATION

Reassessment is rather standard as an early sign of the crisis. Our mid-life man is standing at a time when he is not all future. He has already lived out much of that future toward which he looked as a young man. He will re-examine his goals, his philosophies, his methods of carrying out his ambitions, and his whole value system. He is now forced to consider the man he might have been and the man as he sees himself to be as compared with the man he plans to be.

Identity Crisis

As a result of his reassessment he is apt to suspicion that both business expediency and family trends have made him a prisoner much like a vending machine. He may rebel when he sees what he thinks others view him to be compared with what he really wants to be. Who am I? Where am I going? Will I get there if I stay on the route I am traveling now? These are only a few of the questions which will frequent the mind of the mid-life man.

Loss of Confidence

My mind goes back to a counseling period I once had with a man. He was looked upon as the paragon of success among the radio voices in our city, he was admired by thousands. But he came to me with deep lines of concern etched in his face. He was developing a fear of the microphone that had been his livelihood for years. I didn't really understand what he was going through until years later I noticed, in the beginning of a crisis period, I began to question my own abilities as a preacher.

Such loss of confidence prevails, not necessarily because of a decline of efficiency, but because of an increasing need of reassurance not being met.

The mid-life pilot may notice a strange erosion of confidence as he lands his jumbo jet.

The mid-life preacher may question his overall abilities as he contemplates on Saturday Night his Sunday Morning preaching schedule.

The mid-life salesman may sense a slippage in his confidence with a customer.

The mid-life author may, even after several best-sellers, come to doubt his abilities of communicating anything of substance.

Loss of Discipline

The problem of loss of confidence may be one of the culprits which contributes to a loss of discipline. But all the others previously mentioned may also be suspect. The fact that everything seems to be happening so fast contributes to a disorientation in which old habits long adhered to are abandoned. This brings about an interaction between these conditions which has a tendency to intensify and complicate rather than relieve the problems.

Unreasoned Fears and Anxieties

In this clash between fantasy and reality there are often unreasonable phobias. Some of the above problems precipitate fears of being disabled, of being replaced by someone younger, of dying, or of losing mental capacities.

Forgetfulness

When you awaken to a telephone call in your hotel room and can't remember what town you're in, or begin to introduce your wife to a business associate and forget her first name, look out! It isn't the fear of total amnesia that bothers us as much as the embarrassing silliness of forgetting the most elementary matters. There may be one consolation in forgetfulness. After all, we have more to remember than when we were young. Our batting average may not be too far off after all!

A SENSE OF FUTILITY

With the confusing feelings of the mid-life years the what's-the-use-of-it-all? feeling is apt to come. The thought of a mountain retreat, a remote island in the South Seas, or the little farm back home are more and more appealing as permanent arrangements. The what's-the-use-of-it-all? feeling may then give in to the let's-get-away-from-it-all conclusion.

JOB DISSATISFACTION

There's no occupation on the earth which doesn't have its drawbacks. We may envision the job someone else has as being the ideal, but if we were in their shoes we might quickly be convinced otherwise. I have the ideal calling. I have time to do what I most want to do, that which is most exciting, and that which I feel best equipped to do. I get to travel across the world and meet the most refreshing people on earth. I have the one I love best, Barbara, at my side most of the time. And yet there are some things that I'd still omit if it were my choice.

The mid-life man is apt to zero in on the disadvantages of his occupation and fantasize about pleasures awaiting him after a change in professions.

ANGER AND IRRITABILITY

"My husband has begun to have the disposition of a grizzly!" declares one wife of a mid-life man. This may be a drastic change from the mild-mannered, easy-going, "teddy-bear" he used to be. Inner confusions, feelings of inadequacy, and pressures from several directions bring about a pressure-cooker potential which can be set off by the slightest of provocations.

SEXUAL FANTASIES

The mid-life man may question, along with all the other forces in his life, his love for his wife. He may have experienced a change in his sexual desires. His refusal to face his own aging processes may cause him to reject his wife's aging. He then may find her less attractive and alluring than before. This could result in an undue notice of other women. The mid-life crisis is famous for the frequency with which the "other-woman" affairs develop and occur.

SPIRITUAL DISORIENTATION

As the mid-life man reviews all his relationships and values, his own religious and spiritual relationships are included. Former spiritual zeal may wane, church attendance may let up, and his prayer disciplines may erode.

Guilt feelings may play a vital role in these processes. If he is not aware of what is going on, there may be a chain reaction of discipline breakdowns, guilt, and reactions which will result in a deeply backslidden condition.

This is by no means an exhaustive list of mid-life conditions. There are others which are just as common, but most of them can be categorized under one of the previous headings. It is now vital that we know *what not to do* and *what to do* when we reach mid-life.

SUGGESTED THOUGHTS FOR THE
MID-LIFE MAN

1. *Review the chapter in this book on communication* (Chapter 10). Keep the lines of communication open. Be honest about your feelings during the mid-life period. Your wife should be your chief counselor. Give her attention by deliberate choice and not just when you feel strongly about it. Don't forsake the wife of your youth. Many homes break up during this time. In fact, between the years of 1970 and 1977 there was an increase in divorces by 50 percent among couples who had been married more than twenty years! Stay close to your wife.

2. *Continue with your present profession.* Don't give in to the "middle-aged flight from the rat race." Continue to take vacations at needed intervals, even though you may be enjoying them less and less. If you must consider a job change, give as much deliberation as possible to it. No decision as important as this should be made suddenly. Don't go looking purely on the basis of dissatisfaction with the present situation. Seek the guidance of God.

3. *Get a good, sound physical checkup.* If there are problems they will be exposed. If not, you will be reassured as needed. The worst thing is to be in doubt about it all. Recently I submitted to a full physical checkup at the Cooper Clinic in Dallas, Texas. The result was a small volume of information on all aspects of my physical life. I cannot describe to you the sense of well-being which resulted from the few hours in the clinic.

4. *Establish a discipline of eating, rest, and exercise.* Often a physical checkup will be accompanied with directions in all these areas. Running, walking, golf, tennis, bicycling, swimming, or any one of a number of other exercises will help. A

minimum of such exercises three times a week will keep the mid-life body from undue deterioration.

5. Please remember that this is an era through which you are passing, not a destination at which you have arrived. It is not terminal. It is, in the words of James Dobson, an "unpaved section on the highway of life." Better roads are ahead. It may last as briefly as three months or span more than a year (or more!) However, it will pass! Just as it stole in like a thief, one day you will awaken and it will be gone. The change may be rather imperceptible, but it will pass. You will then begin to look back over the episode with thanksgiving and some amusement. If you are deceived by the myth of permanency you may be tempted to do something which you will regreat for years. The fact that "it came to pass" may be the supreme consolation of the whole crisis.

> Once in Persia reigned a king,
> Who upon his signet ring
> Carved a maxim true and wise,
> Which, when held before the eyes,
> Gave good counsel at a glance.
> Fitting words and these are they,
> Even this shall pass away!

> *Anonymous*

6. *Go on! Continue with life.* Don't stop to look around. This mid-life crisis is a curve, so keep on going until the road gets straight. There was once a missionary who had a poetic bent. One of his converts admired that poetic flair and brought the missionary a poem he had crudely put together. It read:

> Go on, go on, go on, go on,
> Go on, go on, go on, go on,
> Go on, go on, go on, go on.

The amused missionary continued to read, and you can guess what the next lines of the poem contained. It may be poor poetry but it's great philosophy. Go on!

7. *Be honest enough to seek help when you need it.* Don't let pride rob you of help when you need it most. Feel free to discuss your problems with intimate friends. You will find that those of comparable age will be able to identify with you and help you. Others will be helped by your honesty. Don't try to be an island isolated from the mainland of human concern.

8. *Continue to relate to God during this period, even if it is largely a matter of the will.* You may be bereft of spiritual feelings (whatever they are), but you still have your will intact. With your will choose to stay upon God. Read his Word, even when you don't notice any appreciable or immediate edification coming from it.

> Who is among you that feareth the Lord, that obeyeth the voice of His servant, that walketh in darkness, and hath no light? Let him trust in the name of the Lord, and stay upon his God. Behold all ye that kindle a fire, that compass yourselves about with sparks; walk in the light of your fire, and in sparks that you have kindled. This shall ye have at mine hand. Ye shall lie down in sorrow.

Now allow me to draw some profitable conclusions from that passage. I believe they'll be profitable to you.

A. It is possible for a God-fearing, obedient servant of the Lord to walk without sufficient light.

B. In such a time he is to trust in God and stay upon him.

C. In such a time we may resort to lighting our own fire and seeking to light our darkness with the sparks of our own doings.

D. This will be disastrous and will result in our lying down in more sorrow.

So, my friend, <u>go on doing what you did before, even though all your heart may not be in it</u>. Listen to the preaching, even when the storms are raging inside and you are honestly wondering whether the preacher is telling the truth. Go to the Bible study, even in the midst of honest doubt. Have prayer with your wife and family, even when you feel as if your own prayers are not going beyond the roof of the house. Let this be your determination:

> Our feelings come and feelings go,
> And feelings are deceiving.
> My warrant is the Word of God,
> Naught else is worth believing.

> Though all my heart should feel condemned
> For want of some sweet token,
> There is one greater than my heart,
> Whose Word cannot be broken.

> So, I'll trust in God's unchanging Word,
> Till soul and body sever,
> And though all things shall pass away,
> His Word shall stand forever.

Selected

HUSBAND, LISTEN!

Now, in the light of all you have read in this chapter, you may find it hard to believe that, even in the midst of such a crisis, you can still be a loving husband to your wife. You can still meet her needs and allow her to be a part of meeting your needs. Your better understanding of yourself will help you better to understand her in the changing stages of her life. You will become sympathetic to needs even she does not understand. You can learn to be open and honest with her in all relationships. Determine to make this period in your life one of learning, enlargement, and productivity. I have only one suggestion as far as a project is concerned for this chapter. Discuss with your wife those things in this chapter which seem pertinent to you and your feelings.

13
WILL YOU LOVE ME
WHEN I'M OLD?

GROW OLD ALONG WITH ME...
THE BEST IS YET TO BE

The processes of aging are in themselves critical enough. When external problems are added to these the level of severity rises. With such changes the question will inevitably surface on the part of your wife, "Will he love me when I am not physically attractive—when I get old and wrinkled?" Despite the fact that you will be seeking to cope with crises of your own during aging, you must maintain a sensitivity to your wife's special and seasonal needs. You must anticipate the question before it arises and answer it before it surfaces. If the question is voiced before there is conclusive proof that your love is unconditional, the problems of this season will be accentuated.

WHEN DOES OLD AGE BEGIN?

This is an impossible question to answer because there are so many varying factors involved. Old age is largely a state of mind, as well as a cultural entity.

Where children are involved, their leaving the home marks a critical stage in the life of a marriage. In fact, at this point thousands of marriages are terminated because of the inability of the couple to achieve harmony and balance after the children leave. Many of the problems that have been "sleepers"

144

during the life of the marriage, when the children were growing up, awaken when the children leave. For instance, if there has been little or poor communication between husband and wife during that period, the resulting problems can often be compensated for by the wife's total preoccupation in the lives of the children. But when the children are no longer there the problems are exposed. Coupled with menopausal adjustments and mid-life pressures, these often prove too much for the marriage, and the strain reaches breaking point. If available knowledge and resources are not utilized the result will likely be tragic.

At this point the problems connected with aging first begin to be noticed on a large scale. If there has not been some vital preparation made for this time, it may prove to be a period of much heartache for both husband and wife.

DEVELOPING THE SOLUTION BEFORE THE PROBLEM

While the principles within this volume will work in every stage of marriage, it's best to apply them from the beginning. Yet, don't give up if after years of marriage you are just discovering some of these truths for the first time.

Wise men consider eventualities and make preparation for them. A wise husband will anticipate his wife's needs, as he learns of them, in advance and commit himself to be immediately available with the answer when the question surfaces, "Will you love me when I'm old?" Here are some considerations that a wise husband will make as he anticipates the needs of his wife:

1. *Caring enough to continue to communicate.* This must be more deliberate as time goes along. Its importance does not diminish but escalates with age.

2. *Establishing a record of thoughtfulness.* No memory arouses more doubts and insecurities as that of thoughtlessness. A wife cannot help emotional hangover from forgotten special events or badly handled crises.
3. *Compiling a catalog of precious memories.* In addition to being simply enjoyable, the things that a husband and wife do together compile a catalog of memories that are priceless "until death do you part." A walk together in the morning hours, a drive through the multi-colored autumn forests, the sharing of a good book together on a cold day, and special ways of saying "I love you!" are only a few of the items in the catalog of memories which will be beneficial.

Young husband, it is never too early to begin building memories. Middle-aged husband, there is yet time to begin your volume. Older husband, it is never too late!

THE STORY BEHIND A SONG

You have doubtlessly heard the song, "Believe Me If All Those Endearing Young Charms." Have you ever heard the story behind its writing?

Thomas Moore was in a foreign land absent from his wife for a lengthy period of time. During this period his wife contracted a serious disease which left her severely disfigured and scarred. Because she didn't want to complicate his anxieties over being separated from her, she omitted telling him of her illness and of her resulting disfigurement. She also feared that her scars and disfigurement would alter his love for her. As the time neared for Moore to return home, a friend took upon himself the responsibility of informing him by letter of his wife's illness and its grim results. When Moore read the letter about

his wife's problems he sat down and wrote his wife the following letter in poetry:

Believe me, if all those endearing young charms
Which I gaze on so fondly today,
Were to change by tomorrow and flee in my arms
Like fairy gifts fading away;
Thou wouldst still be adored as this moment thou art,
Let thy loveliness fade as it will;
And around the dear ruin, each wish of my heart
Would entwine itself verdantly still.

"When age or illness has taken my human beauty, will that
change your love for me?"

A PERSONAL TESTIMONY

I well remember the days when I almost resented my youth.
I was always thrust among people older than me. I finished
high school at the age of fifteen and college at the age of nine-
teen. I thought I would never get "older." It happened rather
suddenly! I awakened one day, and I was not young any more.
I was not old, but neither was I young.

Barbara and I have been married more than a quarter of a
century. Tammy has finished college and married. Tim will
soon be through college. They are gone! We were faced with a
crisis/opportunity, and it turned out to be plenty of both.

After the crisis of adjusting to being alone with each other
for the first time in more than twenty years, we have moved
into the "best years of our lives." The "empty-nest" syndrome
has eased by us, and we have begun a honeymoon that will
last for the rest of our lives! We are implementing the concepts
and principles of this book, and our love is blossoming more
beautifully than ever.

Maybe we are understanding for the first time the sentiments behind the poignant poem by Robert Browning:

Grow old along with me!
The best is yet to be;
The last of life for which the first was made;
Who saith, "A whole I planned;
Youth shows but half; trust God: see all, nor be afraid!"

EXAMPLES TO LIVE BY

John Wesley was still preaching daily with eloquence and power when he was eighty-eight.

Alfred Lord Tennyson wrote "Crossing the Bar" when he was eighty.

At this writing Vance Havner, over eighty, preaches virtually every week in revival meetings and is doing some of his greatest work.

J. P. Smith, a member in my church, worked in the church nursery until he was past ninety and lived to be one hundred.

My friend, Bertha Smith, ninety-three at this writing, is planning her schedule years in advance, as well as enlarging her effective prayer retreat ministry in Cowpens, South Carolina.

John D. Rockefeller prepared to die at sixty-five, started giving away his millions, and enjoyed it so much he lived to be past ninety.

Ronald Reagan was elected president of the United States as he neared the age of seventy.

Paul Billheimer wrote his classic on prayer, *Destined for the Throne,* at near eighty and received a new ministry for himself and Mrs. Billheimer in their eighties.

Friend, there is life after fifty! and sixty—and seventy—and ... Husband, just because your skin wrinkles your brain does not die. Live on! Think young! Love your bride of years ago more intimately, more energetically, and more devotedly than you did on the honeymoon. Accept the fact of age but don't be morbid. Stay young in heart without being silly. Spend enough time looking back to thank God for his faithfulness, but enough time looking forward to anticipate that which is "best to be." Love your wife with the intensity you would have if you knew it to be your last day on earth with her. Love her with the deliberateness that you would have if you knew yourself to have a hundred more years with her.

Thus, whether you have one year or ninety more together, you will have lived life to the fullest, saying in more ways than one, "Grow old along with me, the best is yet to be."

A PRAYER AS I GET OLDER

Lord, thou knowest better than I that I am growing older, will someday be old,
Keep me from getting talkative, and particularly from the fatal habit of thinking that I must say something on every subject and every occasion.
Release me from craving to try to straighten out everybody's affairs.
Make me thoughtful, not moody, helpful but not bossy.
With my vast store of wisdom it seems a pity not to use it all, but thou knowest, Lord, that I want a few friends at the end of life.
Keep my mind free from the recital of endless details; give me wings to get to the point.
Seal my lips on my aches and pains. They are increasing, and my love of rehearsing them is becoming sweeter as the years go by.
I ask for the grace enough to listen to the tales of others' pains. Help me endure them patiently.
Teach me the glorious lesson that occasionally it is possible that I may be mistaken.
Keep me reasonably sweet; I do not want to be a saint;

some are hard to live with, but a sour old person is one of the crowning works of the devil.

Help me to exact all possible fun out of life. There are so many funny things around us, and I don't want to miss any of them.

Anonymous

14
HUSBANDS PRAYING WITH THEIR WIVES

LET US EXALT HIS NAME TOGETHER

I recently spoke to a group of men about their responsibilities to their wives. I named among these responsibilities that of leading out in prayer with their wives. That evening after the meeting a wife walked up to me. She reported that her husband had come home from that meeting and prayed with her for the first time in over twenty years! I would like to believe that this is a rare report, but unfortunately I am afraid that this is nearer to the rule than the exception.

I was recently asked this question in a marriage seminar: "Why do we husbands find it so difficult to pray with our wives and so easy to pray with other people?" I pondered that question before I made an attempt to answer it. My first thought was, *How true was the fact conveyed by the question!* There was a time when I found it much easier to pray with other preachers or staff members than with my wife.

I want to be honest as I answer this question. Fairness will dictate that I leave a margin around the claims to follow. First, it may be that husbands find it difficult to pray with their wives because they never have. To do something new in the marriage is unnatural and difficult. The margin I leave here, to avert outright condemnation, is that no one informed the husband for more than twenty years. In my memory I cannot

151

recall one instance, before or after my marriage, of anyone informing me that I should lead out in praying with my wife. But I must admit that this first reason does not satisfy me as a thorough explanation. In fact, I am not even sure that this is among the leading hindrances.

I believe, in fact, that the real culprit lies within the atmosphere of the marriage. Every marriage has an atmosphere. It is an atmosphere which is the composite of all the relationship's facets. All the feelings and perspectives of the husband and the wife make that atmosphere one of joy, trust, and liberation or one of sadness, distrust, and stress.

When a husband has to act out of accord, out of "synch," with the normal atmosphere of the marriage, what he does is unnatural, and all who engage in it feel uncomfortable. So it is with praying together as husband and wife. If the atmosphere of the marriage, which is set by attitudes and habits of conduct one toward the other, is not conducive to praying together, then both are forced into actions that seem somewhat unnatural. The result will be, in most cases, that the uneasiness of praying together will dictate that both can conveniently do without it. The answer here is not in giving up but in yielding areas of the marriage to the Great Physician for healing. As God brings two lives into spiritual unity, real praying will be more the natural result and outcome than a forced duty.

WHEN A HUSBAND DOES NOT PRAY WITH HIS WIFE

A husband may ask, "Just how important is it that I pray with my wife?" I am going to leave that answer until after the brief discussion which follows. I believe that the answer will be inherent in the discussion. In a previous chapter on communication I wrote that a wife was always receiving data for her computer. In fact, all of us are doing that. A part of our memory contains what we *heard* each other say. Much more has to do with what we *assumed* each other said by things done and left undone. So, some of the most important things we say are not said with words but with deeds. Praying is one of these indispensable actions. Let me list some of the things a wife might read into the failure of her husband to pray with her:

1. My husband doesn't believe I am spiritual.
2. Others are spiritually more important to my husband than I.
3. My husband isn't interested in my spiritual growth.
4. My husband doesn't have time for me.
5. My husband doesn't consider me a part of his spiritual life.
6. We don't have an "our" relationship with God, only "his" and "hers."
7. My husband doesn't desire real spiritual leadership in our home.
8. My husband is shirking his spiritual leadership.

Now, husband, you might check these matters with your wife to see if these feelings are in line with those of many wives. Husband, what do you want to say to your wife? Your answer to that question will in itself be the answer to the importance of your leading her in meaningful prayer.

Now, for encouragement, let's consider the other side and discuss what is communicated when a husband leads out in praying with his wife. Here are some things that a wife might be "seeing" her husband say when he prays with her:

1. My husband recognizes me as a spiritual entity.
2. My husband acknowledges my spiritual importance.
3. My husband has genuine interest in my spiritual growth.
4. My husband has time for me.

5. I am a part of my husband's spiritual life.
6. We not only have a "his" and "her" relationship to God, but we have an "our" relationship.
7. My husband desires to have spiritual leadership in our home.
8. My husband is tending to his duties as spiritual leader.

PRINCIPLES RELATING TO HUSBANDS AND WIVES PRAYING TOGETHER

Aside from building up the marriage, generating trust, and opening the relationship to the miracle power of God, praying together as husbands and wives cooperates with thrilling principles in the spiritual realm. Here are some of those principles.

There is first the principle of communication. No exercise within the framework of marriage renders the marriage atmosphere more conducive to clear communication than praying together. It alleviates pressures, releases the capacities of love, and implements the relationship of the marriage to God. But there is another matter to remember at this point—namely, that praying together creates an atmosphere conducive to communication, and it is communication of the highest caliber. In the very act of praying together a husband and wife are communicating trust, faith, and love. A few minutes of praying together in the middle of a deadlocked argument can transcend the effectiveness of hours of substantive discussion. It may, then, be said that praying together is the crowning aspect of the whole process of communication in marriage.

Indispensable also is the principle of transparency. My friend, Don Miller who teaches prayer seminars across the country, uses the illustration of magnifying glasses, one imposed over the other, to signify the ministry of husbands and wives praying together. If the husband and wife are to magnify the Lord together in their lives, like the magnifying glasses, they must be clear and transparent. It is at the point of prayer that petty things tolerated will loom large and form obstacles to praying with effectiveness. Their lives must be clean from sin and smudges. The slightest matter on the surface of the magnifier will limit the work of magnifying.

Next, there is the principle of agreement in prayer. In Matthew 18:19 we read, "Again I say unto you that if any two of you shall agree on earth as touching anything that they shall ask, it shall be done for them by my Father who is in heaven." What a promise! There is no evidence that this agreement is confined to any category of participants. We then may assume that this especially applies to husbands and wives, as well as to all other believers.

For our discussion we will study it from the standpoint of marriage. We husbands have more opportunity to prove the validity of this promise with our wives than with anyone else. The evidence that Jesus may often have made this declaration is present in the word "again." Thus, we have a clue to its importance. Everything Jesus said was important. When he repeated a word it was *extremely* important. The action described in this promise is "agree on earth as touching anything they shall ask." The word "agree" is interesting and is more involved than is the English word. The Greek word is *sumphôneô* and is made up of two Greek words, *sum,* meaning "with," and *phôneô,* meaning "to sound." So the literal meaning of the word is to "sound together." It implies more than simple agreement. It suggests corporate pursuit. The word "symphony" is derived from that very Greek word. The designation "anything they shall ask" leaves the situation wide open to the sovereignty of God. We have observed the action prescribed. Let us see the result promised. It is simply put, "It shall be done for them by my Father who is in heaven." The language of this promise-principle is certain and clear! May God help us to employ it as husbands and wives!

The next principle to be considered here is that which concerns the promised presence of the Lord Jesus. The verse which follows the one dealing with the principle of agreement treats the presence of Jesus. In Matthew 18:20 Jesus says, "For where two or three are gathered together in my name, there am I in the midst of them." Though this promise applies to anyone who will take advantage of it, it should be utilized on a regular basis by the husband and wife. The presence of Jesus always makes the difference. A husband and wife can gather in prayer in his name and have the glory of his presence with all its potentials for their home.

I am thinking now of the law of unity. When God took the rib from Adam's side and created woman, Adam's declaration was that they two would be one flesh. Paul recognized this as he quoted from Genesis 2:24 in Ephesians 5:31, "For this cause shall a man leave his father and mother and shall be joined unto his wife, and they two shall be one flesh." When a man or a woman prays alone, not all of him or her prays. There is a lack. There is a God-recognized unity which makes their praying together spiritual business of the highest sort. One God-ordained entity representing the first and oldest institution on the earth is then asserting its highest privilege, namely doing business with the executive offices of all creation! When they pray together, however much they may pray alone, there is a dimension reached in the spiritual life not attainable otherwise. There are chords struck in the unseen realm not heard at any other time. In praying together there is a satisfaction and a strength not reached in any other exercise.

When any two of God's children pray there are remarkable spiritual equations working in the spiritual realm. But when a husband and wife pray there are these equations and more. There is recognized in heaven a hint of the untouched glory of the original intentions. The glory of unfallen Eden is touched again. The vast potential bound up in the bliss of the King and

Queen of Eden is approached once again. I cannot help but think that the devil, the subtle saboteur of marriage, wags his head in utter panic when a married couple exercise this right privilege of prayer together.

When one person prays there are results. When two persons pray the results increase astronomically. I call this the law pertaining to the graduated dynamics of numbers. In Leviticus 26:8 we have a glimpse of this principle when God says, "And five of you shall chase an hundred and an hundred of you shall put ten thousand to flight...." In Deuteronomy 32:30 the same seems to be true on the reverse side when God withdraws His blessing. "How should one chase a thousand and two put ten thousand to flight, except their Rock had sold them, and the Lord had shut them up?" When a husband prays with his wife he is utilizing the spiritual law regarding the graduated dynamics of numbers. If the praying of one causes the devil anxiety, two praying, especially the husband with his wife, sets the evil one in panic!

One man reports, "My wife and I have been married for twenty years, but this morning we had our first family worship together. We sort of stumbled through it, and were both sort of self-conscious, but when we said *Amen,* we just threw our arms around each other, and God seemed to open the windows of heaven and glory came upon us. It was the greatest joy of our married life. Now we know that the greatest privilege of married life is to worship God together in Jesus' name!"

If the truth were known, the titanic battles lost over moral and spiritual issues first began to be lost in the prayerless home. It may be that the final conflict which strikes down a biblical conviction was fought, and lost, in a public arena, but when the final evidence is known the erosion will have first started in our homes. Before modernism and liberalism began to take the altars out of our churches, the devil subtly took them out of our homes!

If the foregoing claims are true, then the path back to biblical morality and godly standards may well be at the reconstructed altar in your home and mine. Whatever our problems seem to be, the seeds from which they have grown were planted in the home. Then with determination let us repair to our homes and begin to reclaim lost ground. There is not a better place, if there is another place at all, to begin than with the husbands of this country calling their families to prayer.

Husband, let me suggest that if you could for a moment imagine all that goes on when you lead your wife and family in prayer, you would surely waste no time getting at it! Something happens in your own heart. God honors a man who will stand in his place as a spiritual leader. He becomes a man in the ultimate sense of the word. Something happens in the heart of your wife. I am not even sure that it can be explained. There is a thrill that occurs in the heart of a wife that surpasses every other pleasure. Buying your wife a Rolls-Royce automobile could not possibly afford more immediate and lasting pleasure than your determination to become her prayer partner.

Permit me to make some elementary suggestions about husbands praying with their wives:

1. Begin now! Don't wait!
2. Pray regularly. Choose a time when both of you have time to spend with each other in prayer. Husband, it's up to you to maintain this time.
3. Develop the art of suggesting prayer at various times when you both are under pressure, when discussing others' problems, when the children have problems, when there is a misunderstanding or any other crisis time.
4. Discuss your own prayer burdens with each other and pursue your own quiet time apart from each other.
5. When you are geographically apart, use the phone as a

means of praying together. A few moments of prayer together when far apart cements a relationship against temptation.

6. Share prayer promises together and rehearse the times through the years when God has wonderfully answered your prayers.

7. Think big and pray big. Widen the circle of your praying to the whole world, current issues, and public officials, and international episodes.

15
ASSESSING THE STRENGTH OF
YOUR MARRIAGE

HOW'S YOUR "M.Q."
(MARRIAGE QUOTIENT)?

Sometimes the worth of a book is greatly enhanced or eclipsed by how it is terminated. We have entertained facts that are little-known and others that are common knowledge. We have waded at times in the shallows of simple considerations and at times have been neck-deep in sophisticated and intricate information vital to the success of marriage.

As much as I would like to have the feeling of thoroughness, that feeling generally proves elusive. I have barely scratched the surface. But I am convinced that enough has been written that, with determined application of even part of it, will strengthen a marriage.

I have been in the process of preparing this volume for more than a year. This is not my general habit in writing. In this case it was both providential and productive. It has afforded me time to step back and look at the work, and has afforded God time to confirm many of the truths herein in our own marriage.

It hasn't been easy. In many respects this has been the greatest year of stress in our fifty-four years of marriage (She has twenty-seven and I have twenty-seven years of marriage experience!). It has also been a year of unprecedented breakthroughs in our marriage. Our feelings are deeper for each other than before. Our patience with each other is more unflagging than *ever* before. Our honesty is more apparent and rewarding. Our communication is more evident and more exciting. God has allowed many areas of consideration in this book to be worked out in the crucible of our relationship. It has been a laboratory of love under pressure. Our mutual assessment is, "It works!" The truth always does its job when given the chance.

During a visit to the Northwest part of our United States, Barbara and I met a lovely couple, Fred and Margaret Luke. They reside in the Seattle, Washington, area. I have asked them for the privilege of sharing something of the work they have done in the field of marriage relationships. They have put together a marriage acrostic which forms the procedure I am going to suggest that husbands use in assessing the strength of their marriage. (Wives might want to do the same!)

> Motivating one another to seek God
> Accepting one another
> Respecting one another
> Responding to one another
> Identifying with one another
> Attentive to one another
> Going in the same direction
> Excited about one another

MOTIVATING ONE ANOTHER TO SEEK GOD

The highest calling of marriage is the same as the highest calling of being a human being, i.e., to know God. When Jesus was asked what was the greatest commandment in the law, he replied, "Thou shalt love the Lord, thy God, with all thy heart, and with all thy soul, and with all thy mind. This is the first and great commandment" (Matt. 22:37-38). Jesus was saying that love is life's bottom line. It's what life is all about. Loving God and one another forms the foundation for all of life's imperatives. If this is not being accomplished through the union of two lives to a greater degree than was true as single people, the marriage is failing or is destined to fail.

Questions such as follow should be entertained by every husband:

1. Do I help my wife to focus on her life purpose?
2. Do I help my wife keep her priorities, i.e., God, self, family, ministry, by:
   A. My use of time or
   B. Accountability for expressed goals or
   C. Other?
3. Do I let my wife know when I see God working through her or in her?
4. Do I pray with my wife in such a way that she is motivated to seek and know God better?
5. Do I help my wife see God's goodness and faithfulness during times of difficulty?
6. Do I share with my wife the things that God is communicating with me?

ACCEPTING ONE ANOTHER

If there is something about your wife you cannot accept just as it is, then you really don't have the kind of love necessary to make a marriage relationship work. Unconditional love is the only kind of love that has redeeming value and is capable of making a relationship successful. In the terms of biblical love it suggests a covenant commitment which is anchored to unconditional acceptance.

Ask the following questions of your relationship with your wife:

1. Do I encourage and comfort my wife when weakness is exhibited?

2. Do I show tolerance or deference for the personal preferences of my wife?
3. Do I try quickly to restore harmony with my wife after there has been an episode of a difficult nature?
4. Do I readily ask my wife's forgiveness and just as readily forgive her when she asks my forgiveness?
5. Do I thank God for every aspect of my wife?
6. Do I share with my wife how she specifically meets needs in my life?

RESPECTING ONE ANOTHER

God has given the responsibility to each party in the marriage relationship to honor or reverence his or her mate. Unless things are done God's way, there is no chance of accomplishing God's purpose. When Peter suggests in 1 Peter 3:7 that the husband give honor unto his wife he used a word which means "to esteem" or "to affix great value." We respect both things and persons on which we have placed great value.

1. Do I express to my wife and others the reasons why I appreciate her?
2. Do I consider my wife's thoughts as important as my own in making decisions that effect the both of us?
3. Do I allow opportunity for my wife to share by referring others to her?
4. Do I honor my wife by:
   A. Not using humor (sarcasm, exaggeration, etc.) about her or
   B. Allowing her to speak in public without correcting her or
   C. Building on to what she says?
5. Do I share my own weakness with my wife?
6. Do I show special appreciation with my wife on special days (such as birthdays, anniversaries, etc.) or at other

times by gifts, cards, notes, flowers, candy, and other surprises?

RESPONDING TO ONE ANOTHER

Marriage is not a 50/50 proposition. It takes 100 percent of all that a man is and 100 percent of all that a woman is. The ideal goal is that of meeting every need of your spouse. This will not be possible without total responsiveness on the part of both. While a woman is more responsive by nature, a man must work at acquiring a responsive relationship with his wife.

These questions will help you in this area of assessment:

1. Does my wife have to ask me to do something more than once before I do it?
2. Do I dominate conversations with my wife?
3. Do I encourage her to ask questions for clarification of what I have said?
4. Do I consistently ask her for suggestions about how I might grow or change?
5. Do I do things that she suggests?
6. Do I handle conflicts in a manner that is acceptable to her?

IDENTIFYING WITH ONE ANOTHER

The coming together of two persons into a marriage relationship means becoming one. You and your wife together make one. Without a continuing awareness of this, it is easy to drift apart and begin to act as two instead of one. It is more than a matter of putting ourselves in each other's place. It is learning to think from there (where we already are) all the time. We two are one. That is our new and true identity.

Meditate on these questions:

1. Am I quick to introduce my wife in social or public meetings?
2. Do I physically identify with her in social or public settings (touching, staying near, etc.)?
3. Do I try to identify myself as a married person when I am alone in a public or social setting?
4. Do I give most of my attention, praise, and interest to her rather than others of the opposite sex when I am in a social or public setting?
5. Do I quickly defend her or rush to her rescue in a public or social setting when she has made a mistake or shown a weakness?
6. Do I plan and participate in activities I can do together with her when participating in an activity with which she is not familiar?

ATTENTIVE TO ONE ANOTHER

We pay attention to what we treasure. Where a man's treasure is, there his heart will be, according to Jesus. That is a simple law. Innate within the character of love is concentrated attention. "My husband doesn't pay attention to me!" is often the plaintive cry of the forlorn wife. While women are more prone to be attentive to persons, men are often more prone to be more attentive to things. The husband, with some determination, must seek to acquire the habit of attentiveness to his wife.

These questions will help you to determine where your real attention is:

1. Do I readily respond with joyful attitudes to tasks my wife wants me to do?
2. Do I do more than what is asked of me in performing these tasks?

3. Do I consistently help her without being asked?
4. Do I allow her to serve me?
5. Do I continue to serve her when she does not acknowledge my serving or when I am treated like a servant?
6. Do I do tasks that are normally done by my wife?

God doesn't draw two people together into a marriage relationship to walk separate paths. He gives them the same desires and motivations about how these are to be fulfilled. Amos, the prophet, asked a long time ago, "Can two walk together, except they be agreed?" (Amos 3:3).

1. Have I discovered as a man my own spiritual direction?
2. Have I conveyed this direction to my wife?
3. Have I lived with her in such a way as to fulfil that spiritual direction in both of us?
4. Do I have agreement with her on the style of ministry desired to fulfil this spiritual direction?
5. Do I agree with her about the place of the church in this ministry?
6. Do I agree with her on how much time I should spend in ministering to others or how much time she should spend in doing the same?

EXCITED ABOUT ONE ANOTHER

The icing on the cake in a marriage is the emotional and physical attraction which exists between a husband and a wife. The unique privileges provided therein are not to be abused or ignored but thoroughly enjoyed within the marriage. Love, properly nurtured, eternally retains its capacity for excitement. Questions such as these should be considered:

1. Do I give and receive affection easily at the appropriate moments?
2. Do I appropriately use endearing names for my wife?

3. Do I take care of my own body (diet, exercise, hygiene, and rest) to give my wife an attractive mate?
4. Do I show sensitivity to her sexual needs and desires by expression, as well as self-control?
5. Do I share my delight with her in her individual physical attributes?
6. Do I plan and prepare for times of intimacy?

Look again at the marriage acrostic:

Motivating one another to seek God
Accepting one another
Respecting one another
Responding to one another
Identifying with one another
Attentive to one another
Going in the same direction
Excited about one another

With determination and prayer, begin to implement these privileges and responsibilities. The results may astound you!

NOTES

Introduction
1. Howard Hendricks, *God's Blueprint for Family Living.*
Chapter 1.
1. John Brown, *Exposition of I Peter* (Marshalton, Del.: NFEA Publishing Company, n.d.), pp. 227-228.
2. *Ibid.*
Chapter 2.
1. Donald Grey Barnhouse, *The Invisible War* (Grand Rapids, Mich.: Zondervan, 1965), p. 45.
2. *Ibid.*
Chapter 3.
1. Alfred Lord Tennyson
2. Matthew Henry
3. Alfred Lord Tennyson
Chapter 4.
1. Tim Timmons, *Maximum Marriage* (Old Tappan, N. J.: Fleming H. Revell, 1976), p. 78.
2. Quoted in William Barclay, *The Daily Study Bible, The Letters of James and John* (Philadelphia: Westminster Press).
Chapter 5.
1. *Pulpit Commentary,* Volume 44 (London: Spence, Wilcox, and Follett, n. d.), p. 375.
Chapter 7.
1. From a tape, "Male and Female Differences," by Eddie Eggerichs. Used by permission.
Chapter 8.
1. J. Allen Peterson, *The Marriage Affair* (Wheaton, Ill.: Tyndale House, 1971), p. 285.
2. *Ibid.* pp. 287-290.
Chapter 9.
1. David Augsburger, *Caring Enough to Confront* (Glendale, Cal.: Regal Books, 1973), p. 3.
2. *Ibid.*
3. Timmons, *Op. cit.*, p. 86.
Chapter 10.
1. Cecil Osborne, *The Art of Understanding Your Mate* (Grand Rapids, Mich.: Zondervan, 1974), p. 67.
2. *Britannica World Language Dictionary.* p. 274.
3. David Augsburger, *Cherishable: Love and Marriage* (Scottdale, Pa.: Herald Press, 1971), p. 49.
Chapter 11.
1. Notes from Bill Gothard, "Advanced Institute of Basic Youth Conflicts."
2. Betty Coble, Woman: Aware and Choosing (Nashville, Tenn.: Broadman Press, 1975), p. 51.
3. Osborne, *Op. cit.*, pp. 55-71.
4. Gary Smalley, *If He Only Knew* (King of Prussia, Pa.: R. M. Marketing Company, n. d.), p. 22.
5. Truman Dollar, *The Role of Women in the Bible* (Printed Material), p. 3. Used by permission.